THANK GOD
in ADVANCE

THANK GOD in ADVANCE

A Companion to the Album

DR. DIANA WILCOX

TATE PUBLISHING & *Enterprises*

Thank God in Advance
Copyright © 2011 by Dr. Diana Wilcox. All rights reserved.

No part of this publication may be reproduced, stored in a retrieval system or transmitted in any way by any means, electronic, mechanical, photocopy, recording or otherwise without the prior permission of the author except as provided by USA copyright law.

Scripture taken from the *Holy Bible, New International Version*®. NIV®. Copyright© 1973, 1978, 1984 by International Bible Society. Used by permission of Zondervan. All rights reserved.

The opinions expressed by the author are not necessarily those of Tate Publishing, LLC.

Published by Tate Publishing & Enterprises, LLC
127 E. Trade Center Terrace | Mustang, Oklahoma 73064 USA
1.888.361.9473 | www.tatepublishing.com

Tate Publishing is committed to excellence in the publishing industry. The company reflects the philosophy established by the founders, based on Psalm 68:11,
"The Lord gave the word and great was the company of those who published it."

Book design copyright © 2011 by Tate Publishing, LLC. All rights reserved.
Cover design by Leah LeFlore
Interior design by Christina Hicks

Published in the United States of America

ISBN: 978-1-61777-561-1
1. Biography & Autobiography / Personal Memoirs
2. Music / Individual Composer & Musician
11.07.25

Dedication

I would like to dedicate this book to my wonderful husband, Walter, for his great faith in Jesus Christ and in our marriage. Thank you, Walter, for growing with me as we walk through life together. I'd also like to dedicate this book to my marvelous daughter, Sylvia, for her exuberance for life, and to my amazing mother, Katya, for her insightful and compassionate approach to humanity.

Table of Contents

PART ONE: MY TESTIMONY

Can Jesus Christ Heal You Emotionally?	11
A Bit of My Story	17
Hope for You	49

PART TWO

Songs of Healing	57
Who is Your Sanctuary?	61
Twin Towers of Gold	69
Have You Done a Double Knockout Today?	75
Are You Wearing a Cloak of Compassion?	83
With Jesus You Can Overcome Your Obstacles!	91
Have you Thanked God In Advance?	97
Do You Know That Peace Awaits You?	103
Do You Dwell In the Secret Place?	107
Is There Is a Larkspur Glen in Your Soul?	115
Are You a Musician of Silence?	123

Injustice to Sweet Justice	129
Green Is My Love Eternal	135
Prayer for the Tinman	139
It's Our Time	143
Angels Fly through Heaven	147

PART THREE: FREE AT LAST

God Uses Broken Pieces—Come Broken	149
Praise God the Father of All Comfort	153
Fall In Love with Jesus	155
Live to Please God	159
Take Care of Jesus's Bride	161
Walk the Walk—Practice Self-Discipline	165
Forgive as He Forgave You	171
Bless Your Abusers	175
Sing a Song of Praise and Joy	177
Humbly Serve Others	179
Put on the Armor of God	183
Overcome Fears	185
Develop Your Spiritual Gifts	189

Study the Bible	191
Pray and Journal Daily	195

PART FOUR
Journal And Workbook Excerpts	197

PART FIVE
Pulling It All Together	297

PART SIX
Receive God's Vision For Your Life	301

PART SEVEN
Sing a New Song to The Lord	305

PART ONE: MY TESTIMONY
Can Jesus Christ Heal You Emotionally?

My answer is yes, absolutely! How do I know? Because He's done it for me! This book complements the CD *Thank God in Advance* and is about how to overcome emotional trauma through a deeper relationship with Jesus Christ. It discusses my emotional healing after years of physical, emotional, and sexual abuse and psychiatric illness. It is my hope that this testimony about my Christian walk will help and encourage you to build a closer relationship with God, the Father of all comfort. Please note that my testimony is in no way meant to disrespect my dearly beloved mother and father, my former husband, or any other person who has been significant in my life. It's only my intention to share with others how my own true suffering was overcome by a relationship with Jesus Christ. I hope that the truths expressed in this book will eventually lead to a better and closer relationship with Jesus Christ for all involved. I deeply thank all the people who have been in my life, for without them I would not have the close relationship that I do with Jesus today. I want to especially thank Anne Graham Lotz, who helped give me the fresh glimpse of Jesus that spurred me to write this book and to begin singing again!

Now I am getting up early nearly every morning, reading my Bible, and writing in my prayer journal. This time with Jesus absolutely rejuvenates me! I have a wonderful life. I am a Christian singer-songwriter and an author. I love performing for people and giving my testimony. I wake up every day with the excitement of another opportunity to serve the Lord. I seek direction from the Lord every day, and He guides me every step of the way. It is very amusing, because in the past few months my friends have been asking me, "What on earth is different about you?" One even asked if I had just gotten back from a vacation to Hollywood. Another asked if I was taking a new medication. I just had to give credit where credit was due and tell them that I am getting plenty of vitamin "J"—Jesus! I am truly spending more time with the Master! My life is not perfect by any means. There are days that are challenging to me, but with God on my side, they never get the best of me. The joy of the Lord is always in my heart. My life was not always this way, however.

A couple months prior to writing this book, I had a dream that I was sitting down and several people were walking around me making fun of me. Suddenly I started flying up into the sky. I was flying up in the sanctuary of my church near the stained glass windows. Suddenly the ceiling of the church turned into thousands of stars, and I flew up into the sky. I believe that the dream reflects the fact that I have been through so much suffering that I have a tremendous amount to share with others. However, I have had a hard time up until now coming up with the words to express my testimony. It is my hope, however, that this testimony will glorify the name of Jesus Christ and help others in similar circumstances.

Part of the reason that it's been so challenging to give my testimony is that I have been through so much that it is hard to know where to begin. Another reason, however, is that, I am not a wordy person by nature! I am shy by nature and have worked to overcome much of my shyness. As a child and young adult I used to be so shy that I hardly wanted to speak. I am mildly autistic. It is as if my volume is turned up a little higher than normal and sounds and colors seem more intense. In addition I have also been hospitalized several times for manic episodes. I have had a few depressive episodes as well and was diagnosed with Bipolar Disorder, which was then relabeled as Schizoaffective Disorder. The label, as well as some people's reactions to it, have been challenging for me to handle in the past. However, I have asked God to help me use all of this to glorify him and to help bring comfort to others.

My parents divorced when I was three years old. I love my mother very much, and we are close now. However, when I was growing up, she was simply was not equipped with many of the skills she needed. I honestly believe she did the best she could with what she had at the time. Although I went through some very challenging times growing up, my mother has helped me over the years in times of crisis when no one else could or would. She is the kind of person you can count on to be there in times of trouble. She is a real survivor! She has cried and apologized to me for certain things that occurred when she raised my brother and me, and I have more than forgiven her. I became interested dream interpretation through my mother, Katya Walter, Ph.D., who is a bonafide expert at this. She has studied in depth at Carl Jung's Institute in Zurich and has led a weekly dream interpretation group for many years in Austin, Texas.

My father, Gary Huddleston, M.D., a very smart, thoughtful, and quiet man, committed suicide when I was seventeen. He was a psychiatric resident at Case Western University at the time. I admired him a great deal.

I have a Ph.D. in Clinical Psychology from the University of North Carolina at Greensboro. I practiced as a psychologist for 12 years teaching, doing research, and doing private practice. Now as a Christian singer-songwriter, I have released a CD called *Thank God In Advance*, which complements this book. In Part Two of this book I explain how the songs on this CD provided me comfort and extra insight into the plan that God has for my life. I am also the mother of three wonderful children, two of whom live in Pennsylvania near their father, and one who lives in Texas with my husband and me.

A Bit of My Story

I first came to Jesus when I was 6 years old watching a Billy Graham Crusade on television at my Grandmother Evans' house in Waco, Texas. I watched the entire crusade. At the end of the program, Dr. Graham turned and spoke to the camera. He told me to get down on my knees and to ask Jesus to come into my heart, and I did exactly that! I felt a warm glow come over me, and I was amazed! I was astounded that the Lord of all creation had come into my soul just like Billy Graham had said he would! I was changed forever! On September 11, 2009, I attended a "Just Give Me Jesus" conference led by Billy Graham's daughter, Anne Graham Lotz. It was so inspiring that since then I have been getting up early in the morning, studying my Bible, and spending more time with the Lord in prayer. That extra time with Jesus spurred on by Anne Graham Lotz is what gave me the inspiration to write this book and to start singing again! Once again the Graham family has had a fantastically powerful impact on my life! I am so grateful for them! I wish I could say that I had been right with God all my life ever since I was six years old, but I took a very long and circuitous path to get where I am today.

Part of the reason it took me so long to come to Christ completely is that I did not grow up in a Christian home. In fact we were not even allowed to have a Christmas tree! One time in particular, when I was about eight and my brother was four, my mother told us that we were not going to have a Christmas tree. I had other ideas, however. I had my eye on the Christmas tree in the school cafeteria! While all the other kids were laughing and talking in the cafeteria, I was contentedly eyeing my new Christmas tree. I knew that all the decorations on it would come off, but I had an idea that once the holiday came it would be by the dumpster, and I would take it home! The last day of school came, and I went to the dumpster, but there was no Christmas tree! I was not going to give up, however! I walked several blocks, asking directions to another elementary school, and there at their dumpster was a beautiful Christmas tree! I carried it home with the help of another kid. My brother was thrilled when he saw it! We didn't have a stand for it so I found a hammer, a nail, and a rope. Then I stood on a chair and tied the rope around the top of the tree and hammered the rope into the ceiling. It worked! There stood the tree! It was glorious! Then we got out some aluminum foil and made a star for the top of the tree! My brother and I danced around the tree singing Christmas carols. It was truly one of the best memories of my childhood—until my mother arrived that is! She was furious and made us throw the tree out by the side of the curb. My mother is happy to have a Christmas tree in her house now, however! In fact, after reading this book, my mother bought me a beautiful big Norfolk pine for a Christmas tree.

I was pretty lonely as a child. It took me quite some time to learn how to relate to people. There were many days when no one at home or school would ask me how I was or would really talk to me. I stayed in my room a lot. I had a stereo and listened to music a lot. I especially liked the Stylistics' song "God Bless You, You Make Me Feel Brand New," Elton John's *Yellow Brick Road* album, Stevie

Dr. Diana Wilcox

Wonder's *Songs in the Key of Life*, Carol King's *Tapestry* album, and the Beatles' *Let It Be* album.

One happy time I remember is picking flowers in a nearby field and making daisy chains out of daisies, Indian paintbrushes, and thistles and putting them like crowns in my hair. I felt close to God then. At night, after things were so chaotic during the day, I would imagine that I was sleeping in the palm of God's hand in outer space, with Saturn spinning and all the planets and comets whizzing by. It was a tremendous comfort to me. I would also walk to a nearby church, where I sometimes played the guitar during the service. I wrote my first two songs around that time, at age nine.

Looking back my brother and I often did not have enough food or basic toiletries. Somehow I did not really realize that this was unusual. I just did the best I could.

When my brother and I used to go visit his father, Bill, and his new wife, Chris, she taught me about transcendental meditation based on Hinduism and gave me the mantra "light." I practiced meditating. Just the fact that she cared so much about me made a big difference in my life. When I was about fourteen, I started going to a mainstream Christian church with another girl from school. I was only able to go on Wednesdays for dinner, choir practice, and youth group. I didn't have anyone to take me on Sundays. It was very helpful and meaningful to me, but the message did not completely sink in. This was probably because I was always in such a state of shock by everything going on at home. During the course of my growing up, I was sexually abused by my mother's boyfriends, date raped, and also physically abused. I wish someone at that time who was a Christian had come to me and been able to give me some guidance then. Do you know a kid like this? Do you have the courage to reach out to them? It could make all the difference for them.

One time when I was about sixteen, my mother took my brother, her boyfriend, and me all on a fascinating trip to Cozumel. I remember walking behind the Mayan ruins and seeing a young girl about my age and height dressed in traditional native clothes. I wondered what different lives we had. I started thinking about my life and what I wanted in my life. There on the Cozumel beach something wonderful happened. I was all alone on the beach and wrote out a prayer to God in the sand like a giant SOS. First I drew a huge heart. Then I drew in it a big cross with a treble clef symbol and a dollar sign. It was my prayer to have a career one day in singing about my love of God!

That same year my mother decided to leave Waco and received a two-year creative writing fellowship at the University of Texas at El Paso. I was on partial scholarship at a private high school where you could work at your own pace, so she told me to finish both my junior and senior years in one year. My brother was twelve and got a full scholarship to a private school just outside of Austin. I finished my junior and senior years in one year, all except a health and a P.E. credit, which I made up by working at a fitness center when I got to Austin.

When I had barely turned seventeen, my mother bought me a $200 Ford Galaxy and pointed me in the direction of Austin, Texas, where I was to go to the University of Texas. Being completely on my own, with no guidance, I missed the deadline for the first semester at UT and went instead to Austin Community College. I worked as a salesperson at a fitness center and a concierge at the historic Driskill Hotel.

In February of my seventeenth year, my father committed suicide. I was absolutely devastated. It was like losing him all over again. After my parents' divorce when I was three, he had come to visit me at various times, and I felt very close to him. Looking back he really didn't visit me very often, only two to three times per year for just a few hours each. He also did not keep in touch with me by phone. He seemed to have a challenging time expressing his feelings towards me, but I knew he loved me.

He had been a psychiatric resident at Case Western University when he died and had planned to come back and work as a psychiatrist in our hometown. He had developed grand mal seizures due to a brain tumor or an aneurism, and these seizures had caused him to hit his head, which in turn caused brain damage. I believe that he lost some of his memory and medical knowledge. I can only guess that the brain damage also caused some emotional and psychological problems too.

As I started college, I went to a yoga class where a friend gave me the book *Autobiography of a Yogi* and started getting me involved in attending a Hindu sect called Self-Realization Fellowship (SRF). It is a Hindu religion that supposedly acknowledges Jesus as one of its prophets. This reminded me of the transcendental meditation that I had done as a child, and I was also entranced by the music in the services. Somehow it didn't occur to me that this was not at all compatible with Christianity. Again, Jesus distinctly says, "No one comes to the Father except through me" (John 14:6). I had never learned this verse in the Bible and really didn't realize that it was an issue.

I met my first husband, Jordan (I have changed his name for the sake of this book), when I was eighteen at a French club on the first day of classes in my first semester at the University of Texas at Austin. His intelligence and charisma reminded me of my mother and felt like home to me. Jordan was an atheist and was trying to convince me that there was no God and that Jesus was just a man. Our disagreements culminated in a trip to Los Angeles for a convocation at the headquarters of SRF. At that time, I remember praying to God to spare me no experience that would bring me closer to Him

Back at the hotel, Jordan kept trying to deprogram me, not only from SRF but also from believing in God. We weren't getting anywhere talking. Finally we decided to write each other a letter about how we felt, because we were getting nowhere talking. He wrote me a brief note, and I wrote a fifteen-page essay! I woke him up early the next morning, read it to him, and we called a truce. I agreed to get out of SRF if he would agree with me to let me continue believing that God was love and that love does exist! I went and returned all my SRF books to the Convocation, which felt fantastic, by the way, and made a new start! It felt good to be out of SRF, because I was beginning to have doubts about the so-called "divinity" of their guru myself. I am very grateful to Jordan for helping me get out of that cult. I wish he had been a Christian too, but he did the best he could at the time.

Jordan and I graduated in May of 1983 and then got married one week later. It was a whirlwind of activity. We then started graduate school in clinical psychology at the University of North Carolina at Greensboro the following fall. It was a very rigorous scientist-practitioner program. I loved learning, doing research, and seeing patients. My Master's thesis was on the stigmatizing effect that psychiatric labels can have on people's perceptions of clients. The thesis won an award in 1987 from the Women's Special interest Group of the Association for the Advancement of Behavior Therapy. Despite the joy I had for learning in graduate school, life seemed empty. If only we had had Jesus Christ at the head of our household how different things would have been.

We first had our son, Aaron, who we realized was autistic when he was about eighteen months old. Then we had our daughter, Sylvia. It was when Sylvia was about nine months old that I had my first nervous breakdown following mounting stress at home. I stayed living with Jordan for another two years after that in order to be with the children. Finally I couldn't stay any longer. Without Jesus Christ in our lives, we had given up on each other and on our marriage.

The divorce was dreadful. I got a small amount of money, which I gave to a lawyer who was unsympathetic to me. Jordan got the kids and the house. A custody evaluation was done, and since I had already had yet another breakdown by then, the children went to Jordan. One night when I was alone in my apartment the spirit of my father came to me and told me that everything was going to be fine. I could feel him hug me. It was then that the Lord gave me a song that I sang into a handheld tape recorder. I titled the song "Injustice," but several years later I added the last verse of the song, and retitled it, "Sweet Justice."

When I wrote that there was injustice in my life that only God could set right, it gave me a peace beyond anything I had known in a long time.

Around that time I also had a TIA - a Transient Ischemic Attack, which is a stroke-like phenomenon. I went blind for a few minutes during the attack. It was very frightening to not be able to see anything with my eyes open. The only thing I could think of resembling a prayer was the Barney theme song: "I love you. You love me. We're a happy family..." By the end of the song, my vision was restored, and I was so grateful to God. The doctors said that the problem, whatever it had been, was averted. It was around this time that I consulted with a preacher and a priest, followed their advice, and left Pennsylvania for Texas for several months. The preacher told me that even Jesus had to get away to the wilderness for a while.

I lived with my mother and her fourth husband, John, at that time. It was very kind of them to take me in, and they treated me very well. I was more depressed then than I had ever been in my life and was trying to fend off thoughts of suicide. I had had bouts of dark depression before that, especially in graduate school, but nothing like this. It felt like I was literally hanging onto life by my fingernails. I told my mother about my thoughts of suicide, and she told me that I should not try it because I would probably botch it up and end up more miserable as a vegetable. This was actually helpful! She also told me that I didn't have to play the role of the miserable, bereft mother. I could step out of the role. That was extremely helpful too. I'll always know how much my mother loves me by how much she cared for me during that time in her own way as best she could. She has a great capacity for kindness, probably because she has been through so much herself. During that time I spent a lot of time writing in a notebook, "I want to live" over and over again.

Eventually, I diagnosed myself as bipolar and got a phone book to call a psychiatrist. I called and was connected with an MHMR clinic. There they gave me Lithium and within a few hours of taking it, I already felt somewhat better. I no longer felt as if I was hanging on by my fingernails. Within a few days, I felt much better. I can't tell you how grateful I am that God gave us modern medicine! I'm not sure how I would have made it without my medication. If you have a mental illness, I urge you to stay on your medication and have it regularly evaluated by a qualified psychiatrist. I also encourage you to see a good Christian counselor. As I got better, my mother also encouraged me to get a job at a nearby bakery and coffee shop, which helped pull me out of my depression.

Determined to be with my children, I finally moved back to Philadelphia. I took a number of acting courses and ended up being cast as an extra in several movies, including playing a nun in Denzel Washington's film, *Fallen*. I had to give Denzel a skeptical look on a train. Being dressed as a nun prior to the filming of the scene was the most comfortable feeling I had ever had in my entire life. The dressing room was far away from the set, and I had to walk through the grand lobby of 30th Street Station in Philadelphia in costume on my way there. I decided that since I was in costume, I was going to get into character, and not just walk through there like a slouch. So I made a point of acting like a nun. I tried to walk with authority, but with humility. The reaction I got was amazing! Some people quickly scampered away from me in fear! Others made way for me and practically bowed before me. One person even offered to get me a drink. It was all undeserved, of course, because I was not a real nun, but I felt as if I were finally home! It was one of the best days of my life! I was in touch with my Christianity again.

On the train, on set, I was reading my Bible when the director came up to the assistant director while preparing the shot and looked at me and whispered something. I was really getting into the Spirit while reading the 23rd Psalm. The director then went away and came back and whispered something again to the assistant director. Finally the assistant director very gingerly came up to me in all due respect and whispered to me, "Excuse me, are you a real nun?"

I said, "I am for today."

He got very nervous and upset and said again, "No, I really mean it, are you a real nun?"

Then I answered, "No, I'm a psychologist." He seemed relieved, but I'm glad that I put the fear of God in them for a moment!

Around this time, I had written a couple songs and had heard that Philadelphia had one of the best recording studios in the country, Sigma Sound. I called, told them that I was not obnoxious, made them laugh, and somehow got an appointment with their president. It was pretty intimidating with all the gold and platinum records up and down the walls! As I walked into the actual recording studio, I could feel a presence behind me almost like royalty. There sat Bunny Sigler. I didn't know who he was at the time, that he was famous for singing "Come on Baby Let the Good Times Roll," or that he was a Grammy-award winning songwriter and producer; I just knew that he was someone special. We talked about our love of Jesus, and he sang his rendition of the 23rd Psalm for me, and we became friends. I am very blessed to be able to have such a good friend as Bunny. He introduced me to Bryant Pugh, the music minister of Sharon Baptist Church in Philadelphia. Bunny began producing the songs for my CD *Thank God In Advance*, and Bryant did all the musical arrangement for the CD.

I was smart enough to start attending a Christian church in Ardmore, PA and started bringing my children there. We were all three baptized there. Even though I attended a Protestant church, and also Catholic mass, I was in complete denial about premarital sex being a sin and did not realize that I was supposed to give all areas of my life over to the Lord. Even if I had ever been told this, it had never registered. I was not smart enough to look for a Christian boyfriend who was committed enough to get married. My life still lacked direction in many areas.

Once, I attended a funeral with Bunny, where I heard him sing. After the funeral I got lost on the way home. I was hungry too, but only had a dollar in my purse. I was hoping to find a McDonalds and get something on their dollar menu. Sure enough, I passed right by a McDonalds and started to go through the drive through. God told me, however, to actually go in and to take my Bible with me! I thought this was nuts, but I obeyed what God said. As I walked into the very busy McDonalds a hush came over the place! Why? What was going on? It was the same exact feeling of being at home that I had as when I was dressed like a nun for the film *Fallen*. I suddenly realized that I looked like a preacher! I had on a black skirt and a white lace blouse and a black Bible in my hand.

God said to me, "Diana, you are going to be a preacher."

And I said, "But God, I can barely talk!"

"That's what Moses said!" God replied. (This was before I even knew the Bible well enough to know that Moses really did say that!) God continued, "Look around at all these people. They need someone to give them the good news. Look into their eyes. See their loneliness and their pain. You have to help them." I ordered and sat down, and God told me to open my Bible and read as I ate and to pray for the different people there. That's what I did, and I felt a peace come over me.

I still didn't get the message to change my life, however. I moved in with my so-called fiancé in Delaware, which was a big mistake. When I finally realized that he was not interested in marrying me, I called my mother. Like a real trooper, she came all the way from Texas and helped me move out. I was still in private practice there in Delaware, but was very lonely. It was farther from my children, even though I still saw them regularly. I started attending an African-American Christian church and sang in their gospel choir. That was one of my fondest memories. I remember having a dream of sitting in church holding a man's hand. I felt that that was a promise from God that would some day come true. During this time in reality I was very depressed and prayed to God asking if I would ever be married to a man who really loved me and cared for me. He answered me! He said, "His name is Walter, and he's been waiting for you a long time." I was confused, because I didn't know any Walters, except my dear friend Walter Bunny Sigler, who was already with someone and was just a friend. I really didn't think much of it after that.

Now of course, I know that my current husband, Walter Wilcox, was my husband to be. I didn't realize the connection until well after Walter and I started dating. It was then that I remembered that God said that he would be my husband. Walter and I had a very challenging first year when I was pregnant with our son Christopher, but we now realize that we were meant to be together, and we have grown closer. Given everything I have been through, I am so grateful now to have a wonderful Christian husband, and a home where Jesus Christ is the head of our household.

Around the time I lived in Delaware I was continuing to take screenwriting and acting classes. I was also involved in taking singing lessons from Bunny and was writing songs. This more artistic direction seemed to be where God was leading me. Bunny Sigler continued producing the songs, and our friend Bryant Pugh continued doing the musical arrangement of the songs.

At one point, I became depressed and threw out all of my medication so that I would not be tempted to overdose with it. Without my medication, however, I eventually became manic and was hospitalized shortly thereafter. At the hospital I saw Jesus before me. He was about six feet tall, but his presence filled up the entire room. His robe was pure white, and he was glowing with golden light. He had long brown hair and an incredibly kind face. He said to me very softly, "Diana, you are going to hell." I said, "No!" I was then led into a room with hospital attendants all around me, but their faces were warped, and they looked like demons trying to grab at me and eat me. I kept saying, "Please don't hurt me. Please don't hurt me." Finally they managed to get a syringe of medication in my arm, and I fell asleep shortly after that. I was amazed to still be alive when I woke up!

Looking back I believe that I had been totally on the wrong track, attending church but not really giving my life or my full tithes to God. I had prayed that God spare no experience that would keep me from being closer to Him, and I got what I asked for. It was the only way He could get my attention. I would like to say that from that moment on

I changed, but I was so thickheaded that it took quite a while longer until I finally devoted my life fully to Jesus.

I went back to Austin to live with my mother. I started dating and moved in with one of my mother's friends who practiced Hinduism, and I got involved in that religion all over again. While meditating at a Hindu service, I had a vision of Jesus calling out to me from every mountaintop on Earth and from every planet in the universe. It was very moving. My mother took me to a drumming circle, and I felt called to start dancing. In the circle I danced for the glory of Jesus. It was a type of prayer for me. I danced at the drumming circles regularly. I also attended an African-American Christian church and sang in their choir. However, I still went to the Hindu and then also Buddhist services to try to please my boyfriend. I even sang my song, *The Larkspur Glen*, for a graduation ceremony at a Buddhist Temple. There in Austin my life was a hodge-podge of religions and philosophies that added up to exactly nothing! Sometimes less is more.

Finally some of my family in Waco came down to Austin and suggested that I consider moving to Waco. They said that we could do things together as a family and that it would be a better place for me. I prayed about it right then and there, and God said that that was exactly what He wanted me to do. At that time I had already applied for social security disability, which was pending. I stayed with them and got on the right medications and then got an apartment. I am grateful to my family for all their help. It was then that I started attending church again and watching Trinity Broadcasting Network day in and day out.

During that time of enormous suffering with my illness, I came across the story of "The Silversmith" by an unknown author. It was an invaluable comfort to me. The story goes like this: A group of women studying the book of Malachi, came across chapter three verse three which says: "He will sit as a refiner and purifier of silver."

This verse puzzled the women, and they wondered what this statement meant about the character of God.

One of the women offered to find out about the process of refining silver and get back to the group at their next Bible study. That week this woman called up a silversmith and made an appointment to watch him at work. She didn't mention anything about the reason for her interest or curiosity about the process of refining silver. As she watched the silversmith, he held a piece of silver over the fire and let it heat up. He explained that in refining silver, one needed to hold the silver in the middle of the fire where the flames were hottest as to burn away all the impurities.

The woman thought about God holding us in such a hot spot—then she thought again about the verse, that He sits as a refiner and purifier of silver. She asked the silversmith if it was true that he had to sit there in front of the fire the whole time the silver was being refined. The man answered yes; he not only had to sit there holding the silver, but he had to keep his eye on the silver the entire time it was in the fire. If the silver was left even a moment too long in the flames, it would be destroyed.

The woman was silent for a moment. Then she asked the silversmith, "How do you know when the silver is fully refined?" He smiled at her and answered, "Oh that's easy. When I see my image in it."

The lesson? Even in the midst of all my suffering, God was still with me. He was watching over me, like a refiner of silver. What the enemy meant for bad, God was using for good. He was using the hottest part of the fire, the worst part of my sufferings, to burn away the impurities in my heart, my mind, and my soul. Even though I sometimes felt abandoned, I knew that God was with me and that He was not going to take His eye off of me. I knew that somehow, my suffering was all for the greater good, and that one day God would be able to start seeing His image in me!

Can you have faith that in the midst of your suffering God is with you? Do you believe that He is watching over you like a refiner of silver? Are you willing to let Him burn away the impurities in your heart, mind, and soul? Do you realize that God has never abandoned you, and that He has always had His eye on you? Are you willing to let God start seeing His image in you?

Say a prayer right now asking the Lord for these things: Lord, Let me have faith that even in the midst of my greatest suffering you are with me. I believe that you are always watching over me like a refiner of silver. Let me be that silver. Dear Lord, I ask that you burn away any impurities in my heart, mind, and soul. Thank you for never abandoning me and for always keeping your eye on me so that I did not fall into the flames and be destroyed! Lord, make me more and more willing each day to let you see your image in me. I long to imitate you. Let me be a pure reflection of you.

I came to Christ fully about seven years ago, at age forty-one, watching the Trinity Broadcasting Network. God arranged it so that it was the only station that my little TV could get! I watched TBN day in and day out, getting saved over and over again, raising my hands and being filled with the Holy Spirit. I really didn't understand that I only needed to be saved once. In fact there is a salvation phone line that I kept calling once a week or so to be saved again and again and finally they asked me to stop calling and told me that I had already been saved! This was a real blessing to me to realize that I really had been saved! I don't know what I would have done without TBN! No one else was reaching into my living room at all hours of the day and night, giving me the kind of ministry that I needed. All of the pastors on TBN became my friends: Paul and Jan Crouch, the 700 Club folks, Paula White, Joyce Meyer, Jentzen Franklin, John Hagee, Bishop T.D. Jakes, and Gregory Dickow.

As I watched TBN and listened to their talk of the happiness of the Christian marriage in particular, I started thinking that maybe if I married a Christian husband, things would work out for me. I also felt that being so very poor and living on disability, I would probably be better off if I were married. I immediately went over to my computer, got on the Internet and looked up "Christian singles" under Google. A little blurb came up that said that many Christian singles apply to American Singles.com. So I filled out my profile on that site, and the first profile to come up, since I mentioned that I wanted a Christian, was Walter. He stated in his profile that he would only date a Christian woman. He looked very kind in his picture and being a physicist, sounded very smart. The only problem was that I could tell from the date on his profile that he never checked his messages! How was I going to reach him? Then it occurred to me that if he was a Christian, a physicist, and lived in Waco, he probably worked at Baylor University in Waco. So I did a little detective work: I got on the Baylor website, went to the Physics Department, and there was the same picture that he had used on the singles website! It was a match! I looked up his email address and emailed him, which was very awkward for me. We met, found out that we were going to different services at the same church, and the rest is history. We now have a wonderful little boy.

One thing I was able to do during my pregnancy was to continue recording some of the songs on the CD *Thank God In Advance*. That was a wonderful experience. I feel so alive when I am in the recording studio singing to God's glory and working with my friends, Bunny and Bryant! While I was staying at my hotel in New Jersey near the studio, I took a walk alone out into a forest full of beautiful yellow flowers. The flowers covered the entire area. I stopped and rested there and prayed to God. Earlier that morning the flowers had all been closed, but now they were open taking in the sun's rays. The Lord told me that my music would reach many people in this way, that it would help them open up their souls and soak up the healing love of the Lord. He told me to look far off into the woods on either side where other yellow flowers were also blooming. He said that people of other nations would also hear the music and be saved. It was a very gentle and profound communion with God.

Reflecting on this vision, I recall an amazing dream I had recently of a beautiful green field with scatterings of orange flowers here and there. Then the orange flowers turned into orange cows and then the orange cows turned into orange Monarch butterflies. I believe that the orange flowers represent the people who are going to increase their faith in Jesus by hearing my music and reading my book. The flowers turning into cows represent those same people's ability to learn to use their new found faith to enhance the faith of others in their own lives. The cows turning into Monarch butterflies represent those people's freedom to enter into the majestic kingdom of God. Just as Joseph explained to Pharaoh about Pharaoh's dream, "The reason the dream was given... in [three] forms is that the matter has been firmly decided by God and God will do it soon" Genesis 41:32.

I have just completed a Bible study developed by Anne Graham Lotz on Revelation called *The Vision of His Glory*. It has helped give me a clearer vision of Jesus. Since attending Lotz's "Just Give Me Jesus" Conference, I have been inspired to get up early in the morning and spend more time reading my Bible and writing in my prayer journal. God has told me that the more on fire I am for Him, the less "on fire" my brain will be in any kind of nervous breakdown. I really do believe that. I recommend that you be on fire for Jesus too! Attending the conference has helped me to overcome my shyness about singing my songs in public and has catapulted me into a new relationship with Jesus Christ and into a bold new singing career. I still have many challenges, but I have a peace and a joy that only Jesus can give. I am truly happy and thank God in advance for all the blessings He continues to give me.

After writing the first draft of this book, I went through a period of depression, because I realized that my disability income would be jeopardized if I made over a certain amount of money each month in my CD and book sales. Through prayer and talking with my pastor, husband, and friends, however, I have decided not to give up my dream! I believe I am doing God's will in marketing my CD and book and any concerns about losing my disability income are secondary. "But seek first his kingdom and his righteousness, and all these things will be given to you as well" Matthew 6:33. If the book and CD are successful, I will no longer need my disability income! Hallelujah! Praise God, and thank him in advance!

I am reminded of Abraham being asked to sacrifice his son Isaac. He offered his son to God, and then in the last minute God provided him with a ram to sacrifice instead. The Lord God, Jehovah Jireh, always provides! I believe that the disability income that I may have to forfeit is my Isaac and that God will provide me with the finances I need to continue my ministry.

Additionally I don't want to be like the last servant in Jesus's parable of the talents (Matthew 25:14-30) who did not use his talent and got his talent taken away from him!

As Jesus has told us, "You are the light of the world. A city on a hill cannot be hidden. Neither do people light a lamp and put it under a bowl. Instead they put it on a stand, and it gives light to everyone in the house. In the same way, let your light shine before men, that they may see your good deeds and praise your Father in heaven" Matthew 5:14-16.

True worship requires sacrifice. What are you willing to sacrifice to God? Is it your time, your money, your pride? Is it some area of your life that you have been reserving only for yourself? In sacrificing something that is valuable to you and stepping out of your comfort zone you will be worshipping God at a new level that you have not been on before. Therefore you will reap rewards that you have never seen before as well.

New and wonderful things are about to happen for you!

Let me tell you an amazing dream I had along these lines. In the dream I was in a wheel chair, wheeling myself around, and then suddenly I decided that I had to do something, so I got up out of the wheel chair and lifted it up and put it somewhere else. Then in the dream I came to some steps leading up to a higher level, and I felt very weak. I saw a young man walking down the steps and asked him if he would help me up the steps, because I was feeling weak, and he did.

I believe that this dream means that I am not as disabled as I think I am. In the dream I am stepping out of my "disability career" and putting it somewhere else. I then come to a higher level and am willing to admit my weakness and ask another person for help. Who is that other person? Jesus! And He lifts me up to the next level!

By sacrificing my "disability career," I was able to go beyond my comfort zone to a new level. It is so easy to stay in our "comfort careers" and play it safe, but God wants us to go beyond that and truly live the lives that he commands us to live. This does not mean that you have to give up whatever career you happen to have. However, it does mean that you might want to examine not just your career, but also your whole life. Are you really living the abundant life in the Promised Land that God has planned for you or are you holding back, walking around and around in the wilderness of your own soul? God is calling you out of the wilderness. Do you hear his call? It's time to get out of status quo, time to get out of mediocrity—you are destined for greatness! Give up your comfort career for a crescendo career!

Hope for You

You may feel at times that you want to give up completely or that things aren't going right for you but think about how much God, the Creator of all the universe, cares for you. When I lost custody of my children I cried a thousand lakes of tears, not just for myself but also for them. Before the divorce, I had a prophetic dream. I dreamed that my first husband's stepfather kicked me out of the house and nailed the front door shut so that I couldn't come in. Then I walked out to the front of the house and looked up at the windows of the master bedroom where I saw the house on fire with my children's faces in agony in the windows, crying for me to let them out. I couldn't get to them. They were in a hell. What could I do? I woke up.

In reality, I really did have to leave the house and really was concerned about my children's spiritual welfare. But guess what happened? My children were refined like gold in God's fire. It still brings tears to my eyes to think about the divorce and my children's undying love for me.

This is a good example of Romans 8:28: "And we know that in all things God works for the good of those who love him, who have been called according to his purpose." My apparent misfortune, as some might call it, has not ruined me or made me bitter. Instead I am using it to buy gold refined in the fire (see Revelations 3:18). That gold is wisdom and love and patience in affliction. I used to feel angry that I did not have custody of my children, but I have given my anger to God, and, in exchange, He has given me white clothes to hide my impurities. At times I've felt blind as to where God is leading me, but with God's word, I've bought salve for my eyes that they may see the truth of God's vision for me.

Yes, that's it—God has a vision for me. And if He has a vision for me, surely He has vision for you. Sometimes I feel angry that I have this ridiculous disorder, and I have asked God to remove it from me, but like He told Paul, He has said, "My grace is sufficient for you, for my power is made perfect in weakness" (2 Corinthians 12:9).

Being on disability, I ask myself what I can do. I pray for God to enable me to do what He would have me do. As Jesus says in John 15:5, "I am the vine; you are the branches. If a man remains in me and I in him, he will bear much fruit; apart from me you can do nothing." If you knew the kind of fruit you could bear with God's help, to what extent would you remain more in Jesus? Would you study your Bible more and spend more time with Jesus in prayer?

Reading further, "If you remain in me and my words remain in you, ask whatever you wish and it will be given to you. This is to my Father's glory, that you bear much fruit, showing yourselves to be my disciples" (John 15:7-8). When you feel disabled, realize that you can do all things through Christ who strengthens you. I confess that I have not always remained in Christ, which is why I began to whither and die and probably why I have seen visions of hell in the past. But I can use those visions for good: I urge you, my friend, turn to Jesus. There is nothing worse than seeing Jesus's kind face telling you that you have to go to hell, as I told you that I have when I was hospitalized. Remain in Christ and do not waver. As the Lord says, "Walk in all the ways that I command you, that it may go well with you" (Jeremiah 7:23). Now that I have completely dedicated my life to Christ, and I have given all of my life to Him, I am free to remain in Him and to bear fruit.

You may ask yourself, if I remained even more in Jesus what kind of fruit would I ask to bear? You will be allowed to bear much fruit only if you put God's glory first. We need to realize that God wants us to wish to bear much fruit as a way of showing that we are His disciples. You may find that God closes a door in your life, but when he closes a door, he opens another. Revelation 3:8 says, " I know your deeds. See, I have placed before you a door that no one can shut. I know you have little strength, yet you have kept my word and have not denied my name." Even if you have little strength, if you keep Jesus's Word and proclaim His name, He will place a door of opportunity in front of you! What door of opportunity is before you that you have not yet seen? Surely your life itself is an open door. Use it to the fullest!

In the past, I have felt many times like giving up, but that would have been selfish. I know that God does have a door open for me. As it says in Jeremiah 29:11, "'For I know the plans I have for you,' declares the Lord, 'plans to prosper you and not to harm you, plans to give you a hope and a future.'" God is your friend and has a great plan for your life. You just need to draw closer to Him in your suffering to see His plan. How patient are you about remaining in the Spirit when you are suffering so that you can hear God's voice? Instead of focusing on ourselves we need to focus on Jesus and His vision for our lives. For His vision is far greater than ours, especially when we compare His omniscience to our myopic pity parties.

My point is that we have to go on! But I don't mean that we must just have to limp along through life, going through the motions like empty shells. God wants us to do more than just survive; He wants us to thrive! Have you ever been depressed? Believe me; I do know what it feels like. During that time, please remember that the Creator of the universe cares very deeply about you. He wants more for you than your just feeling dead inside. As it is plainly written in Revelation 3:1-2, "I know your deeds. You have a reputation of being alive, but you are dead. Wake up! Strengthen what remains and is about to die, for I have not found your deeds complete in the sight of my God." Simply put, if you are still alive, God has not yet decided that your deeds are complete, and if they are not complete, you'd better get on the ball and do them!

How would you live your life differently if you realized to what extent your deeds were not complete in God's eyes? What if there were all kinds of great things you would have been able to do if only you were closer to the Lord? It's not too late! What if you realized all of the many new and wonderful deeds He has planned for you? Would you spend more time with Him then to catch a better glimpse of this vision? Why not do it now? Begin today. That is what I am doing. I realize that in the past I have forsaken my first love of Jesus, and I need to remember the height from which I've fallen (Revelation 2:4-5). I have repented of my sins and humbly asked Jesus to forgive me. I've committed to spend more time with Jesus in prayer and in the study of His Word. I pray to God that you and I both will wake up and stop going through the motions in our lives and be more passionate about Jesus and His Word! I pray that you and I will hold onto our crowns and strengthen our faith in Jesus!

I love Jesus so much that I don't know where to begin. I am like the man who owed 500, rather than just 50, denarii and loved his master even more since he had been forgiven such a great debt. It is my hope that I will be able to offer you some comfort in this book and its companion CD through the comfort that God, the Father of all comfort, has given me during my times of great suffering.

PART TWO
Songs of Healing

This book complements the CD of songs titled *Thank God In Advance*. These songs represent a map of my journey of healing. I thank God for His inspiration for these songs and the great comfort and healing they provided. It is my hope that they will be of tremendous comfort you. Samples of the songs can be found on my website at dianawilcox.com and at soulprodigyministries.com. This section contains notes on each of the songs on the CD in the order that they appear on the CD. I don't feel that I actually wrote any of the songs. God dictated them all to me, and I simply wrote them down or sang them into a tape recorder. I'm just the secretary. I thank God for the inspiration of these songs and my dear friend Bunny Sigler for producing the songs and my talented friend, Bryant Pugh, for doing the musical arrangements for the songs.

Dr. Diana Wilcox

One of the things that helped me to write the melodies for most of the songs is that I sometimes have synesthesia when I write music. Thus I sometimes experience the music as color, and I simply decide how much "deep blue" or "streaks of yellow" I want there to be in the music. When I explained this to Bryant he was very helpful and actually used his amazing talent to add in certain "colors" here and there into certain songs as we worked together.

A few of the songs were recorded when I lived in Delaware and was going through a challenging time there. I had an incredible dream at that time. I dreamed that I was in my apartment, but that my bedroom was a psychiatric hospital room. I dreamed that the only thing in the room was a single metal bed. In the dream I could smell gas, and I was starting to suffocate. It was an emergency, and I had to escape from the room, but the door was blocked. The only way out was the window. I looked down and realized that I was on the second story. I took three sheets off the bed and tied them together to make a rope and escaped out the window! Then I touched the green grass on the ground safely!

The amazing thing about the dream though was that those three sheets were three "sheets" of music—representing the three different songs I had just recorded! These were "Sanctuary," "Prayer for the Tinman," and "Twin Towers of Gold" or as I called it back then, "How to Weave a Harness." In my dream, the sheets actually had lit up staffs of music and notes written on them! I believe that God was trying to tell me that somehow He would use my music to save me! And that's exactly what He did!

This CD was completed in October of 2007, but it was not until 2009 that I began this book as a plan to market the songs. Why the delay? I was holding myself back. Due to my slight autism I felt too shy about singing in public. I also felt that I had to have the words in front of me to sing and felt self-conscious about that. What's more, I was allowing the stigma of psychiatric labeling to get to me. In short I was doing a mental number on myself. Now I realize that, "God did not give us a spirit of timidity, but a spirit of power, of love, and of self-discipline" (2 Timothy 1:7). This means that my spirit of timidity was coming from the enemy. It is important to note that the enemy worked very very hard to keep these songs from being heard! I truly believe that the songs on this CD are so powerful that the enemy does *not* want you to hear them!

Therefore, in the name of Jesus, I refuse to let any autism or psychiatric label or other people's expectations of me keep me from lifting these songs up to the glory of God! If I need the words in front of me, so be it. I am singing it to please God, not to fulfill others' expectations. I ask God to bless those people who don't expect me to succeed, but I can't live my life to please them and suit their expectations. I hereby start living for God, and God's approval alone! In the name of Jesus, I cast out the spirit of fear and negative thinking and replace it with a spirit of love, power, and self-discipline! I pray in the name of Jesus that you, dear reader, will be able to do the same in your own life and that all your dreams will come true!

Who is Your Sanctuary?

Have reverence for my sanctuary, I am the Lord.

Leviticus 19:30B

Sanctuary
Lyrics and Melody by
Diana Wilcox
Musical Arrangement by
Bryant Pugh
Produced by Bunny Sigler
©2007 Diana Wilcox

Sanctuary
In deep dark space.
A light beam's gone astray.
Sanctuary
In deep dark space
A tiny piece of day.
Sanctuary

Dr. Diana Wilcox

In deep dark space
These embers will survive.
Far from the winds of others' words
Who won't keep theirs alive.
They may try to blow yours out
With their own fear
And their own doubt,
But you can shine for miles about
While they just sit and sigh.
Chorus:
Sanctuary
I want to be
Where my heart can fly.
Sanctuary
I want to be
Somewhere
Way way up high.
Sanctuary
Calm me down
Take me into flight.
Sanctuary
Seize my mind.
Spin morning from the night.
Sanctuary
What's that I see?
Looking through the clouds at me?

Thank God in Advance

Jesus from another star!
You caught me from so very far.
Sanctuary
Midnight blue!
Orange sparks in roaring glory!
Intersect, dance, and sing!
Tell each the others' story!
Sanctuary
I'll always be
Where my heart can fly!
Sanctuary
I'll always be
Somewhere way way up high!
Sanctuary
Calmed me down.
Took me into flight!
Sanctuary
Seized my mind.
Spun morning from the night!

A sanctuary, like a bird sanctuary, is a safe place where we cannot be harmed and can thrive. Do you have a sanctuary? Is it your home or your car or a particular vacation spot? What do you do if you have no sanctuary? When I first wrote the song "Sanctuary," I felt that there was some sanctuary far off in the distance somewhere. I had not written the verse about Jesus yet, but I knew that somewhere, somehow, there was a sanctuary with someone greater than myself. I longed to be there in that sanctuary. I was not reading my Bible and was not really even praying to God at that time. I had gone astray and was lost. That is why I wrote, "A light beam's gone astray." Now I know that even in the "deep dark space" of my isolation and loneliness, God was there with me, and He was encouraging me even though I had forgotten how to speak to Him. He told me in the song, "These embers will survive. Far from the winds of others' words who won't keep theirs alive. They may try to blow yours out with their own fear and their own doubt, but you can shine for miles about while they just sit and sigh."

A couple years later the rest of the song came to me, except I originally wrote "angel from another star you caught me from so very far" as if I were writing it to a boyfriend. That was a laugh! That guy told me he would make a contract with me to be engaged with me for five years and then might consider renewing his contract! My girlfriend told me to tell him that I was not a baseball player! Oh how foolish the heart is! I finally left him. He asked for a copy of the song that was dedicated to him, but I decided that he could listen to it on the radio when it came out like everyone else could! I finally went back to the recording studio and my producer, Bunny, was understanding enough to let me record over that part in the song where I say "angel from another star" and say "Jesus from another star" instead. This was very important to me, as I had fallen in love with Jesus all over again, and I realized that the song had been about the sanctuary of Jesus that is inside each one of our hearts all along.

On the day that I started writing this song, I found my inner sanctuary in Jesus, even though I was so distraught that I was not able to call Him by name at the time. In that sanctuary, God gave me a promise that I would be blessed and be "where my heart (could) fly." In Hebrews 6:13-15, God promises to bless Abraham, who waits patiently and is blessed. Just as God's promise to Abraham was fulfilled, His promise to me was also fulfilled. Once I started walking in Christ and devoting my life fully to Him, I got to that place in Christ where my "heart could fly" with joy. "We have this hope as an anchor for the soul, firm and secure. It enters the inner sanctuary behind the curtain, where Jesus, who went before us, has entered on our behalf (Hebrews 6:19-20a)."

Falling in love with Jesus is a marvelous thing! It is indescribable beyond words! Even though I had strayed so many times from Jesus, He "caught me from so very far" as the song says. Then that's when the fireworks went off as if a supernova had exploded in outer space. That tiny ray of light that had been in isolation was finally with Jesus. As the song says, "Sanctuary midnight blue! Orange sparks in roaring glory! Intersect, dance, and sing! Tell each the others' story!" Here Jesus and I were communing with each other as if in a big cosmic dance, singing psalms of praise to God on high! He was telling me all about Him, and I was confessing and repenting and praising Him and telling Him all about me! It was then that I made the commitment to Him, my sanctuary, that I'll always be with Him, "where my heart can fly." Finally, I acknowledged Him as my sanctuary who gave me a sound mind. He "calmed me down. Took me into flight! Sanctuary seized my mind. Spun morning from the night!" As the Psalmist says, "Weeping may remain for a night, but rejoicing comes in the morning (Psalms 30:5)."

If you are going through a challenging time, press in toward Jesus. Seek Him. Seek His sanctuary, and you will find that He will guide you there. Be patient and hang on. Hang on and remain in the Spirit in your suffering. You will fall in love with Him! No person, place or thing can substitute for Jesus. He is the only gate to heaven. He is the true vine and, as He says, "Apart from me you can do nothing (John 15:5b)." Even if you are so distraught that you have forgotten how or don't know how to pray to Jesus, just try and the Holy Spirit will pray for you. "In the same way the Spirit helps us in our weakness. We do not know what we ought to pray for, but the Spirit himself intercedes for us with groans that words cannot express (Romans 8:26)."

Lean in toward Jesus. Jesus has more for you than earthly sustenance; He is Living Water and the Bread of Life. As He said to the Samaritan woman at the well, "Everyone who drinks this water will be thirsty again, but whoever drinks the water I give him will never thirst. Indeed the water I give him will become in him a spring of water welling up to eternal life" (John 4:14). That is a sanctuary—where you never thirst, and you are never hungry. Let Jesus be your sanctuary now and forever. Then you will always have a sanctuary with you in your heart wherever you go!

Twin Towers of Gold

Be still, and know that I am God; I will be exalted among the nations, I will be exalted in the earth.

Psalm 46:10

Twin Towers of Gold (How to Weave a Harness)
Lyrics and Melody by
Diana Wilcox
Musical Arrangement by
Bryant Pugh
Produced by Bunny Sigler
© 2007 Diana Wilcox

Twin towers on a runway
Destined for the flames
Twins, Somerset, and Pentagon
Will never be the same.
But how do you weave a harness
For six billion souls or more
To guide this precious planet past

Dr. Diana Wilcox

The fiery force of war?
Running like the wind
With the finest harness made of gold
Beyond so far beyond
That place where my soul was sold.
Gleamin' in the starlight
Runnin' through the snow
This brave horse, mane runnin' wild
Knows just where I want to go.
But how do you weave a harness?
Of gold as in the dream?
How to I weave my soul and I
Together as a team?
Packhorse treading
through the streets
With its blinders on.
Loaded down with urgencies
From here 'til time beyond. (Jesus)
Once riding on that packhorse
From the corner of my eye,
I spied that great wild stallion
Patiently walking by my side. (Jesus)
The harness turned to love
bright gold as in the dream,
But how do I weave my soul and I
Together as a team?

Thank God in Advance

A glint of gold flashed
through His eyes
And the story then was told
…Weave it of the finest strands
…Of dreams and deeds of gold.
That's how you'll weave a love
Bright gold as in the dream
That's how you'll weave
God's soul and you
Together as a team.
But how do you weave a love
For six billion souls or more?
To wrap around the oceans and lands
Shore to shore?
Alpha, Omega,
Faithful and True
Spirit and Bride
Unite Anew.
Let Twin Towers of Gold
In America
Still Stand
As beacons of love and light
Throughout the land.
Lift up all the world's Children
To trade at towering heights
And reign over darkness

Dr. Diana Wilcox

> With God's golden light.
> Earth spinnin' round
> Shrouded in this love,
> Hear her soft sound in the coo
> Of a Dove.
> Gleamin' in the starlight
> With this love made of gold
> This Brave Horse, mane runnin' wild
> Knows just where we want to go!

I was counseling one of my dear patients in Delaware when the twin towers of the World Trade Center were hit in New York on September 11, 2001. I had an appointment in Manhattan the next week. As I came up from the subway, I could smell the smoky stench that filled the air. Everyone was in shock. People banded together and were much kinder than usual.

I wrote "Twin Towers of Gold" shortly after that. I was very overburdened with work at the time, and I could truly identify with Jesus carrying the cross to His crucifixion. This is symbolized in the verse "packhorse treading through the streets with its blinders on, loaded down with urgencies from here 'til time beyond." And yet I knew that even during the time of His crucifixion, Jesus knew that He was going to rise again and take His place at the right hand of God. Thus I wrote, "Once riding on that packhorse from the corner of my eye, I spied that great wild stallion patiently walking by my side." Even in the midst of the storm of our afflictions, Jesus is always walking by our side.

In the song I ask, "How do I weave my soul and I together as a team?" and the horse, representing Jesus, answers back, "Weave it of the finest strands of dreams and deeds of gold. That's how you'll weave a love bright gold as in the dream. That's how you'll weave God's soul and you together as a team." Here "the finest strands of dreams and deeds of gold" represent our need for God's mercy and our need to follow God's vision for our lives in even the smallest way. The horse corrects the singer—it is no longer about weaving "my soul and me" together, but about weaving my soul and God together. When we make God the center of our lives, we can finally become happy. We must put ourselves aside.

Then the singer asks, "But how do you weave a love for six billion souls or more? To wrap around the oceans and lands shore to shore?" Now that's a different question! Or is it? Not really. Drawing from Revelation, the horse answers: "Alpha, Omega,

Faithful and True, Spirit and Bride Unite Anew." Thus when Jesus comes again in the second coming, He will unite with His bride the church, and there will be peace on earth forevermore. The song continues, "Let twin towers of gold in America still stand as beacons of love and light throughout the land. Lift up all the world's children to trade at towering heights and reign over darkness with God's golden light." The Spirit and His bride are the true Twin Towers of Gold that no one can ever destroy. I played this song for a retired fireman who lost some buddies in 9/11. He was moved to tears and said that he couldn't wait for it to come out!

Have You Done a Double Knockout Today?

I saw heaven standing open and there before me was a white horse, whose rider is called Faithful and True. With justice he judges and makes war. His eyes are like blazing fire and on his head are many crowns..The armies of heaven were following him, riding on white horses and dressed in fine linen, white and clean. Out of his mouth comes a sharp sword with which to strike down the nations. He will rule them with an iron scepter. He treads the winepress of the fury of the wrath of God Almighty. On his robe and on his thigh he has this name written: King of Kings and Lord of Lords.

Revelation 19:11-16

Dr. Diana Wilcox

This is how Jesus will come the second time. And this will be a double knockout!

What is a double knockout? It's when Jesus comes first as a babe and then the second time as a king. He does a double knockout on the enemy!

Double Knockout
Lyrics by Diana Wilcox
Melody and Musical Arrangement by
Bryant Pugh
Produced by Bunny Sigler
©2010 Diana Wilcox

I'm gonna do a Double
Knockout today!
I got so tired of seeing those liars
That I just got up and bled.
I got so tired of see-
ing pagans and thieves
That I just got up and said,
I'm gonna do a Double
Knockout today!
Gonna put that Satan finally away!
Gonna kick that mutt in the butt!
And send him on his way!

Thank God in Advance

Yes, I'm gonna do a dou-
ble knockout today!
Said pagans get over here.
Listen to what I have to say.
You got nothin' to fear
'Less you do it some other way.
Love your God with all your heart,
Not some idol or some nut!
Love your neighbor as yourself
And you just might make the cut!
Cause I'm gonna do a
Double Knockout today!
That's eternity-speak to you!
Come in one day as a Babe
Next as a King – It's true!
You might be thinking
Who is this kid
Talkin' 'bout me so strong
Well, I've been thinkin'
That she's alright and
She's just where she belongs.
Sometimes Jesus speaks
through folks,
Sometimes He does not,
But if rap's what grooves your spokes,
Then satan's gonna rot.

Dr. Diana Wilcox

Cause I'm gonna do a
Double Knockout today!
You've heard 'bout mad as hell?
Well I've been there hun
Ain't no fun,
But to Me it's kinda swell.
Cause some of yous deserve
to be there now
That's where you belong.
Heaven can wait all it wants,
But your stench is way too strong.
Yes, I'm gonna do a Double
Knock-out today!
They nailed Me to a cross!
But that don't stop the One they say
Is really really Boss!
You better stop your lying, cheat-
ing, thieving, stealing ways
And that sexual immorality is
grating on my soul I'm afraid!
So hit and run you number ones!
You preachers, saints, and called!
We're in a battle here, and
you done already falled!
You falled so far I can't see
you - try as though I may.

Thank God in Advance

But Joel Osteen - I tell you what
- He sure brightens up my day!
Put on your armor and get to prayin'
cause prayin' does some good.
And good is what we
need 'round here.
Now is that understood?
My Dad's a little irritated
By some little things you say,
Like could I maybe, sorta, kinda
have things go my way?
For heaven's sake! Pray boldly now!
We're in a war my friend.
He's your Old Man too
don't ya' know,
Until the bitter end.
Folks the end is coming.
It's coming sooner than you know.
And I'm gonna get ya'.
It's coming to a close.
So put on your mercy shoes.
Make that pact of peace.
Try to be friendly now.
Put on some extra grease.
That grease is prayer my friend

> We need it quite a bit.
> So rappity rappiity rap my friend
> Rap this faithful hit.
> It's gonna be a Double
> Knockout, my love,
> Come with Me if you choose,
> We love ALL God's children up here,
> But without Us you're
> SURE TO LOSE!
> KNOCKOUT!!!

The words of "Double Knockout" came to me in the middle of the night as pure dictation. I could barely write the words fast enough. I had recently visited a beautiful rose garden and one of the rose bushes was called "double knockout." That name struck me as beautiful and powerful at the same time, just like Jesus!

It was pretty challenging to do a rap song, but my dear friend Bunny helped a lot with the rhythm, and, of course, Bryant Pugh's music made it all come together. The song warns of the second coming and the need to pray boldly rather than timidly, realizing that we are all God's precious children.

We need to realize that the second coming is just around the corner and live as if the second coming is today! Your mission in life is to gather as many souls for Christ as possible by the example you lead in your life. This is how you as a Christian can do a double knockout on the enemy. Satan does *not* want you to live your life like this! He does *not* want you to live your life to the fullest! He does *not* want you to do a double knockout! Do whatever you can to frustrate him! Have you done a double knockout today?

Are You Wearing a Cloak of Compassion?

Cloak of Compassion
Music by Bryant Pugh
Lyrics by Diana Wilcox
Produced by Bunny Sigler
©2007 Diana Wilcox

There is a cloak of compassion,
Kindness, humility, and grace.
Beyond any other fashion
Wearing it you'll see God's face.
There is a boundless glory
Wrapped in Jesus's love.
Don your cloak of compassion.
Light your world from above.
Put on your cloak of compassion
When faced with darkness and strife.
Patience is God's passion.

Dr. Diana Wilcox

With it He'll grant you long life.
With your cloak of compassion
You never will be charmed.
See them with God's own eyes.
Watch their hearts disarm.
Look through the lies and fears.
Behold my own child's face.
Wounded pains of yesteryear
Lifted from disgrace.
Jesus loves
All who fall
Each foot
Made of sod.
Like toddlers learning
How to crawl
Your greatest
Strength is God.
Put on your cloak of love.
Let it envelop you.
Look into souls from above.
And see them through and through.
There is a great shield
Made of God's pure love
And with the words you wield
You'll entertain angels above.
Mercy now is in their eyes

> As they see you see them.
> Abandoning their own disguise,
> You'll help them live again.
> Walking through life's deserts
> When kindness can't be found
> Never find life's treasures
> Buried underground.
> Forgive as He forgave you.
> Words richly drench your heart.
> Peace rains sapphires of blue,
> Blooms into an art… an art…
> Get your cloak of compassion.
> He's already taken your blame.
> A mantel forever in fashion,
> Bearing The Great Designer's Name.

When I worked as a clinical psychologist in private practice, I sometimes used a strategy from the Bible with my patients of telling them to put on a "cloak of compassion." This strategy worked especially well for patients, such as prison security guards, who had to work with challenging populations of people. It was very effective. The strategy is described in the song, "Cloak of Compassion." I had already written most of the song when I showed the lyrics to my good friend Bryant Pugh. He was able to come up with a gorgeous melody for the song within a few moments. As I worked on writing the rest of the song in a hotel room in New Jersey in preparation for recording it the next day, I used a Gideon's Bible in the hotel room to look up the scripture upon which the song was based:

> Therefore, as God's chosen people, holy and dearly loved, clothe yourselves with compassion, kindness, humility, gentleness, and patience. Bear with each other and forgive whatever grievances you may have against one another. Forgive as the Lord forgave you. And over all these virtues put on love, which binds them all together in perfect unity.
>
> Colossians 3:12-14

The words came automatically while taking dictation from God. I really can't take any credit for the song. God helped me to write, "Put on your cloak of compassion when faced with darkness and strife." When you have compassion for your enemy you see through your enemy with God's eyes, and then your enemy sees that you see him that way and is disarmed. When you are wearing your cloak of compassion, you are wearing "a shield made of God's pure love and with the words you wield you'll entertain angels above." You see when you have on your cloak of compassion and love, you automatically wear your shield of faith, because you are believing God for a miracle right then and there! You will see into your enemy's heart. As the song says, "Look through the lies and fears. Behold my own child's face. Wounded pains of yesteryear lifted from disgrace." We are all precious children of God lifted into His grace. The song also says that, "Jesus loves all who fall, each foot made of sod. Like toddlers learning how to crawl, your greatest strength is God." Jesus loves us in our weakness, and in our weakness we have God's strength.

The song then goes on to say, "Mercy now is in their eyes as they see you see them. Abandoning their own disguise, you'll help them live again." When you obey the Bible and clothe yourself with compassion, you will not only disarm your enemy, you will make him or her a better person. You will find that your enemy abandons his or her own "disguise." As Paul says in Romans 12:17, "Bless those who persecute you; Bless and do not curse." We are to rejoice when our enemies rejoice and mourn when they mourn. "Do not overcome evil by evil, but overcome evil with good (Romans 12:21)."

The song says, "Walking through life's deserts when kindness can't be found, never find life's treasures buried underground." It is important to stay in the Spirit, even through afflictions and even in the face of suffering, to never keep your talents hidden underground. In Jesus's parable of the talents of gold, the master got very angry with the servant who buried his talent (Matthew 25:14-30). God transformed my anger over losing custody of my children and my suffering into a healing balm of songs, but it took me a long time before I realized that I needed to overcome my mild autism and share that healing balm with others.

When I got to the point that I was able to forgive my former husband, I felt a washing peace come over my heart. I was free from my anger towards him and it was Jesus, and only Jesus, who had done that for me. Thus I wrote, "Forgive as he forgave you. Words richly drench your heart. Peace rains sapphires of blue, blooms into an art... an art." The peace that reigned in my heart after I truly forgave my former husband was all encompassing. Here "rains sapphires of blue" refers to the true riches, the true wealth that rains down upon you when you fully accept Jesus Christ into your heart and learn to follow his commands. The wealth of Jesus's love is more precious than silver or gold.

"Get your cloak of compassion. He's already taken your blame. A mantel forever in fashion, bearing the Great Designer's Name." When Jesus died on the cross, He already took the blame for our sins. The little ditty at the end about the cloak bearing "the Great Designer's name" really means a lot to me, because as a teenager almost all my clothes came from Goodwill, and I never had a pair of blue jeans. I remember back then looking at all the girls in my private school with their designer jeans and fur jackets and thinking that they had those things because they needed them and that God didn't give me them, because I didn't need them in order to be happy. Now, whatever I am wearing, I know that if I put on my cloak of compassion I'll always be wearing The Great Designer's label. I was able to finish the lyrics to the song using the hotel room's Gideon's Bible, which was invaluable to me at the time. And thanks again to my dear friend, Bryant Pugh, for the awesomely beautiful melody.

With Jesus You Can Overcome Your Obstacles!

I tell you the truth, if you have faith as small as a mustard seed, you can say to this mountain, 'Move from here to there' and it will move. Nothing will be impossible for you.

Matthew 17:20b

Obstacles
Lyrics and Melody by
Diana Wilcox
Musical Arrangement by
Bryant Pugh
Produced by Bunny Sigler
©2010 *Diana Wilcox*

Obstacles,
I've overcome obstacles.
They were many, and they were few.

Dr. Diana Wilcox

Obstacles,
I've overcome obstacles,
But I could never have done it
Without You.
Oh God, the pain
That I have gained
When I saw
What I'd gone through!
Oh God, how much
I could have crushed
This whole world
Right up in two!
Obstacles
You threw away obstacles.
They were many,
and they were few.
Obstacles
You threw away obstacles.
You just severed
Them right in two.
Oh God, You came!
Erased the pain!
Now I shout for joy anew!
The pain is praise
For the love You gave
And the way

Thank God in Advance

You saw me through.
Obstacles
I understand obstacles.
They were many,
but they were few.
Thank You God,
Thank You for the obstacles,
For they have brought me
Closer to You.
Oh God, You're great!
I have just praise for
Your Name above all Names.
I sacrifice
With shouts of joy
For every little girl and boy
To sing the songs
To whom Your Holy Name belongs!
Jesus, removes our obstacles!
We are hea- heavenly-bound!
Jesus, removed our obstacles!
You can hear it in Gabriel's
trumpet sound!
I sacrifice
With shouts of joy
For every little girl and boy
To sing the songs
To whom Your Holy Name belongs!

You may feel that the obstacles you have keeping you from a good life are too great. However, with Jesus's help you can overcome them. What seems like many obstacles will seem only like a few compared to the great joy you will have when you fully give your life to Jesus, and He reigns in your heart. Obstacles in life are created by our own sin and by the sin of living in a fallen world. In the song I write about the great pain that I have been through. It is wonderful to know, however, that Jesus understands our pain and suffering. He endured far greater suffering in every way.

In the song "Obstacles," Jesus helped me to write that even though I've overcome obstacles, I never could have done it without Him. Jesus turns pain into praise. He erases our sins and our pain and shows us a way through the darkness. Long ago I prayed to God not spare me any experience that would bring me closer to him. And that is exactly what I got. As the song says, "Obstacles, I understand obstacles. They were many, but they were few. Thank you God, thank you for the obstacles, for they have brought me closer to you." Compared to the glorious feeling of being close to Jesus and knowing that I will be with Him for all eternity, the many obstacles I've been through are really few.

I also pray that you, the reader, will sing the songs of Jesus and teach them to the young boys and girls of God's kingdom. As the song says, "I sacrifice with shouts of joy for every little girl and boy to sing the songs to whom your holy name belongs!" I have seen so many children in my work as a child psychologist in dire need of Jesus's teaching, who just need to know that Jesus loves them. I have seen many children who needed to learn about what the Bible says about how to behave. For example there was one particularly mischievous boy who I had write an essay on the Proverbs 10:23: "It is the sport of the fool to do mischief, but a man of understanding hath wisdom." He wrote a good essay, and his behavior improved dramatically!

The song declares, "Jesus removes our obstacles! We are heavenly bound! Jesus removed our obstacles! You can hear it in Gabriel's trumpet sound!" What are our obstacles? Our obstacles are sin. Jesus has died so that our sins have been forgiven by God. When you and I get up to heaven, we will still be sinners, but Jesus will stand with us before God and tell Him that we have been washed in the blood of the Lamb. Our obstacles to our one true goal, God, will be gone. And we will remain with Him eternally in heaven in His kingdom of light!

Have you Thanked God In Advance?

My heart leaps for joy, and I will give thanks to him in song.

Psalm 28:7B

Thank God in Advance
Lyrics and Melody by
Diana Wilcox
Musical Arrangement by
Bryant Pugh
Produced by Bunny Sigler
©2010 Diana Wilcox

Thank God in advance!
For the day is coming!
When you'll take the chance
And stop just humming!
Talk like Him and me
God wants you to be

Dr. Diana Wilcox

ALL that you can be.
It's kinda hard
To talk right now
So step up
And take a bow.
Do you know
How you talk?
The same way
God helps you walk!
Chorus:
Thank God in advance!
Your future is coming!
You'll start to jump and dance
And we'll all be funning!
Autism ain't no fun
No not for anyone.
You got so much
To live!
Such a
Great mind
To give!
The strain you feel
Is your strength.
You can talk
Before you blink.
Stand on up to the plate.

Thank God in Advance

God's gonna do it mighty great!
Chorus:
Thank God in advance!
Your future is coming!
You'll start to jump and dance
And we'll all be funning!
Autism ain't no fun
No not for anyone.
You got so much
To live!
Such a
Great mind
To give!
Aaron, Aaron, Aaron, man
God has for you a steady plan!
Go ahead and try to talk
You know you're smarter
Than a hawk!

Jesus has a wonderful future for you! Yes, He wants to be your sanctuary, but he also wants you to venture out of your comfort zone and see the great plans he has for you. Have you seen them? Draw closer to Jesus and you will. How do you draw closer to Jesus? I have found that by reading and studying my Bible more and communing with Jesus in prayer I can remain closer to Him. "Call to me and I will answer you and tell you great and unsearchable things you do not know (Jeremiah 33:3)." Much of my life I have neglected my Bible reading and, in doing so, neglected to read a love letter from my first love. I had read Psalms and Proverbs some, but that was about it. I was intimidated by the rest, I guess. Probably, I was afraid to read about all the things in my life that I would have to change if I truly intended to follow Jesus. I have asked the Lord to forgive me for these sins. Now I can look back and know that the Bible is not just a book of rules. Jesus is our friend and wants to help us to thrive, and the rules are there to help us be better and happier people. Above all, we have God's grace, his love, and His unmerited favor.

I wrote the song "Thank God In Advance" for my son, Aaron. The song thanks God in advance for the miracle that He is going to do in Aaron's life. Aaron is moderately autistic and speaks in a rote kind of way. The song is a prayer that God will help Aaron to overcome his autism in the same way He helped me to overcome my much milder form of autism. As the song says to Aaron, "God wants you to be all that you can be." This applies to all of us. God has a vision for our lives. Aaron has brought so much joy and comfort into the lives of those he encounters. He is truly a blessing.

The song says, "The strain you feel is your strength." Actually, the strain we feel comes from God's strength, because it is in our strain and our weakness that God is strong. "My grace is sufficient for you, for my power is made perfect in weakness. Therefore I will boast all the more gladly about my weaknesses, so that Christ's power may rest on me" (2 Corinthians 12:9). One of Aaron's greatest gifts is singing. He may not always have the pronunciation exactly right, but the spirit of the song is impeccable and is gorgeous to witness. He has even sung in church before.

Like Paul, I have asked and asked God to remove my psychiatric disorder, the thorn in my flesh, but He has explained that His grace is enough for me and that in my weakness He is strong. Therefore, like Paul, I shall be glad of my weaknesses, for the more I remain in Christ, the more He allows me to bear fruit in spite of or perhaps because of my weaknesses for His name's sake. When you are in Christ, the more you give up the more you have!

Dr. Diana Wilcox

I want to thank God in advance for all the wonderful things He is going to do in my life, for fresh vision of Jesus that He is giving me as I speak. I praise Him for His awesome majesty that cannot be captured in human words, and I praise Him for His humanity. I praise God that I am able to write this, for usually I am a woman of few words! I wonder if I will truly be able to write this book. Yet "We live by faith, not by sight (2 Corinthians 5:7)." So I will keep writing as the Spirit moves me.

Glory Halleluiah! I have just realized that even though I wrote this song about Aaron overcoming his autism and thanking God in advance, it is really about me overcoming my autism and thanking God in advance! I have been so shy that I have not been marketing my CD until now, because I have decided not to let my autism hinder me!

Even though I am shy, I will sing only for God's approval and not worry about everyone else's approval. What a release! "For the day is coming! [I'm going to] take the chance! And stop just humming!" I'm ready to sing! I'm ready to thank God in advance!

Do You Know That Peace Awaits You?

And the peace of God, which transcends all understanding, will guard your hearts and your minds in Christ Jesus.

Philippians 4:7

Peace Awaits You
Lyrics and Melody by Diana Wilcox
Musical Arrangement by Bryant Pugh
Produced by Bunny Sigler
©2010 Diana Wilcox

Peace awaits you golden town.
Peace awaits you love.
Peace awaits you harvest town
Like a Holy white dove.
Peace is surrounding you
Like a golden band.

Dr. Diana Wilcox

Peace is encompassing you
Telling you to look and stand.
Stand up for what
Is right and true
Stand up for what is pure
Stand up for what is
Sweetly made from hands
Oh so sure.
Peace is coming to harvest town
And to gold town too.
It's crossing all the nation's towns,
And I've seen quite a few.
His name is Jesus Christ my friend.
He's the Purest of the Pure,
And the Holy of the Holies
He's coming here for sure.
Watch out for the Peace I'm told
For He is the King of Kings
And with Him comes a love for
His Bride that only
A King could bring!
Peace awaits you golden town.
Peace awaits you love.
Peace awaits you harvest town
Like a Holy white dove.
Peace is surrounding you

Thank God in Advance

> Like a golden band.
> Peace is encompassing you
> Telling you to look and stand.
> Stand up for what
> Is right and true
> Stand up for what is pure
> Stand up for what is
> Sweetly made from hands
> Oh so sure.

I was thinking about Jesus and the peace that passes all understanding when suddenly a deep peace came over me and the song "Peace Awaits You" came to me. This song is a promise from God. Like "Double Knockout," it is about the second coming of Jesus.

The song says that peace is coming to "golden town" and to "harvest town" too. I believe this refers to all groups of people, including big modern cities and small farming communities as well. The peace tells us to "stand up for what is right and true." Then we learn that, "His name is Jesus Christ my friend. He's the purest of the pure. And the Holy of the Holies. He's coming here for sure."

Jesus is sovereign. We learn this in my favorite line of this song: "Watch out for the peace I'm told for he's the King of Kings and with Him comes a love for His bride that only a king could bring!" Jesus loves His church. Do you appreciate your church community and fellow believers? We need to love each other and ourselves as Jesus's bride. We need to realize that we are all part of the body of Christ.

Do You Dwell In the Secret Place?

In Psalm 91, David tells us that, "He who dwells in the shelter of the Most High will rest in the shadow of the Almighty." The song "The Secret Place" was inspired by this Psalm.

> The Secret Place
> Melody and Lyrics by Diana Wilcox
> Musical Arrangement by Bryant Pugh
> Produced by Bunny Sigler
> ©2007 Diana Wilcox

> You will dwell
> In The Secret Place.
> In his shadow
> You will see his face.
> Refuge, strength
> In God we trust.

Dr. Diana Wilcox

Snare of the fowler
Put to dust.
Chorus:
Cover you
With his wings
Shield and buckler
Refuge sings
Do not fear
The sick by night
Nor the arrows
In their flight
Thousand fall
At your side
Ten thousand called,
Will not abide.
You are called
To seek His face
Forever guard you
In His grace
Make the Lord
Your Secret Place.
Nothing come
To take your space.
Watch the wicked
As they fall.
Only you

Thank God in Advance

Will see it all.
Angels watching
Over you
Lift you up
In all you do.
Lest your foot
Dash a stone
They'll carry you
Toward heaven's home.
You'll trample lion under foot.
Tread on cobra in the soot.
You have set your love on me.
Set on high you shall be.
Chorus:
Cover you
With his wings
Shield and buckler
Refuge sings.
Do not fear
The sick by night
Nor the arrows
In their flight.
Call on me
I'll answer you
Deliver you
In all you do

Dr. Diana Wilcox

> My salvation
> Will be yours
> I'll honor you
> Forevermore.

I wrote the song "The Secret Place" originally as a prayer for protection for those who have undergone any kind of abuse or trauma. The song says, "Do not fear the sick by night." This is referring to those who are sick with sin. In Matthew 9:12 Jesus told the Pharisees why He was dining with sinners: "It is not the healthy who need a doctor, but the sick." We are all sick with sin.

The melody came to me at the same time as the lyrics. Later, however, when my friend, Bryant, and I were discussing the musical arrangement for the song, I asked him to depict it as a strong panoramic theme, as if legions of spaceships were going off to do battle with evil. Bryant pulled this off very successfully. As Bryant was playing the music, I thought of the United States and the courage of our service men and women who fight evil around the world. I decided that this would be a good song to send as a prayer for protection to our President.

Thank God in Advance

Below is a copy of the letter I wrote to President George W. Bush:

> Dear Mr. President,
>
> Enclosed please find a CD with accompanying lyrics of a song based on Psalm 91 for you listening pleasure. I am a Christian singer-songwriter and have written this song to give you renewed strength, courage, and a double-portion of fortification in the battle against terrorists. They are real and frightening, and their evil must be stopped. Thank you for your valiant work in leading our nation and our troops against evil in the world.
>
> I pray that this letter finds you in top form, mentally, physically, and spiritually. The word "you" in the Psalm (and in the song) applies to all "who dwell in the shelter of the Most High."
>
> I am a 14th generation descendent of William Brewster, who was the preacher on the Mayflower, and who helped to write the Mayflower Compact. My father, Gary Lee Huddleston, M.D., served in the United States Air Force Intelligence. I, myself, have a Ph.D. in clinical psychol-

ogy and now have a songwriting ministry. I am a native Texan.

I pray that both the music and lyrics of this song, "The Secret Place," minister deeply to you, and serve to renew your spirit.

In Jesus's Holy Name,
Dr. Diana Lee Wilcox

I was very humbled to receive a response back from President Bush thanking me for my correspondence.

This song is also about the battle that will take place between good and evil when Jesus comes again. Malachi 4:3 describes the second coming: "Then you will trample down the wicked; there will be ashes under the soles of your feet on the day when I do these things." This is reflected in the song's line, "Watch the wicked as they fall. Only you will see it all." This scripture is also reflected in the line, "You'll trample lion under foot. Tread on cobra in the soot." The song goes on to say, "You have set your love on me. Set on high you shall be."

Jesus not only provides a sanctuary for us to rest in, but he also provides a secret place from which to do battle. "For our struggle is not against flesh and blood, but against the rulers, against the authorities, against the powers of this dark world and against the spiritual forces of evil in the heavenly realms (Ephesians 6:12)."

Pray with me: Lord, help me to dwell in the secret place, resting in the shadow of the Almighty. Help me to be willing to battle evil in the world for you, Lord, so that I may lay a crown at your feet when I get to heaven. Give me strength, courage, and endurance for the battle as I put on the full armor of God. In Jesus's name, Amen.

Is There Is a Larkspur Glen in Your Soul?

As the deer pants for streams of water, so my soul pants for you, O God.

Psalm 42:1

The Larkspur Glen
Lyrics and Melody by
Diana Wilcox
Musical Arrangement by
Bryant Pugh
Produced by Bunny Sigler
©2007 Diana Wilcox

The Larkspur Glen
Was covered in
Foliage blue and green.
You had the sharpest, sweetest eyes
That I had ever seen.

Dr. Diana Wilcox

Chorus:
Sharper than an arrow,
Sweeter than the moon,
Your eyes glided past me gently
Like a breeze gone to soon,
Like a breeze gone to soon.
Motionless I stood there
'Neath the shadow of a tree.
You turned Your horse around
To come back to talk to me.
Chorus:
Sharper than an arrow,
Sweeter than the moon,
Your eyes pierced into a soul
Larkspur about to bloom
A soul larkspur about to bloom.
Through the glen we flew
With feathers in our hair.
The sun poured 'round the pines.
As we danced without a care.
Chorus:
Sharper than an arrow,
sweeter than the moon,
Your eyes glided past me gently
Like a breeze on high noon
Like a breeze on high noon.

The night fell and the wrens
Did coo themselves to sleep.
We walked together
through the forest
Calm and dark and deep.
Chorus:
Sharper than an arrow,
Sweeter than the moon by far,
Your eyes gazed into my soul
As if irised from a star,
As if irised from a star.
Let's go back again one day
To the Larkspur Glen
For Your soul was the
Kindest place
That I have ever been.
Chorus:
Sharper than an arrow, sweeter
Than the moon by far,
Let's iris both our souls
Up to a new born star.
Up to a new born star.
Up to a new born star.

Do you remember a time when you were head over heels in love with Jesus? Have you forsaken your first love by neglecting your Bible reading or your time with Him? I know I have. I pray that this song, "The Larkspur Glen," will help you rediscover that love, and reclimb the height from which you've fallen.

The song is written to Jesus. The lyrics and melody were dictated to me as I sat alone on the Santa Monica Beach a couple days before Valentine's Day, asking the Lord to help me write a song about love. This song reminds me of the favorite hymn "I Come to the Garden Alone." The garden, the larkspur glen, is the place in our own soul that Jesus invites us into when we have Him in our heart.

According to the song, Jesus's eyes are indescribable. They are "sharper than an arrow" and "sweeter than the moon". They are "sharper than an arrow" because Jesus is omniscient. His eyes blaze into us with all knowledge of everything about us. Yet, at the same time, Jesus eyes are "sweeter than the moon" because they are all forgiving and overflowing in eternal loving kindness, compassion, and mercy. This song reflects God's great majesty in the simplicity of nature: blue and green foliage, a shadow, a blooming larkspur, feathers, a breeze, and a star.

The song says, "Motionless I stood there 'neath the shadow of a tree. You turned Your horse around to come back to talk to me." This reflects how we can be stunned by Jesus's greatness beneath the shadow of the cross. It also shows how Jesus will always turn around and come back to give us a second chance.

The song then continues, "Sharper than an arrow, sweeter than the moon, Your eyes pierced into a soul larkspur about to bloom." The larkspur here is me. Jesus's eyes pierced into my soul as I was about to bloom into my true God-given potential. This is followed by great joy, dancing, and celebration of God's creation in the song. "Through the glen we flew with feathers in our hair. The sun poured 'round the pines as we danced without a care."

I believe Jesus was speaking to me of a time when I was about eleven or twelve and was singing and playing my guitar at church occasionally and fell in love with Jesus. I began to realize that I had a God-given potential and that Jesus loved me. The song goes on to say, "Your eyes glided past me gently like a breeze on high noon." This is about how Jesus's love is like a cool breeze on a hot summer's day. We are desperate for His love, His comfort, and His kindness, and it can all be ours if we just accept Him into our hearts.

In the song, the relationship with Jesus deepens more and more as night falls, and we walk through the forest with Him, "calm, dark, and deep." Then with eyes "sweeter than the moon by far," he gazes into our souls "as if irised from a star." Jesus longs to have a close, loving relationship with you all the days of your life. This is a love song that he is singing back to you too!

Finally, the song says, "Let's go back again one day to the larkspur glen for your soul was the kindest place that I have ever been." You see, when we were children, a part of us remembered Jesus, that kind place. Jesus longs for you to go back to that place in your childhood when you trusted and loved like a child. I believe Jesus is calling to us through this song to come back to be with Him in the larkspur glen of our souls as we did when we were children. Let the child in you come back to Jesus. "Let the little children come to me and do not hinder them, for the kingdom of God belongs to such as these. I tell you the truth, anyone who will not receive the kingdom of God like a little child will never enter it." (Mark 10:14-15).

The song ends by suggesting, "Sharper than an arrow, sweeter than the moon by far, let's iris both our souls up to a new born star." The possibility of sending both of our souls up into heaven affirms the omnipotence of Jesus and how it is only through Jesus that we can go to heaven. The song also speaks of rebirth and transformation. As Jesus states, "I tell you the truth, no one can see the kingdom of God unless he is born again ... Flesh gives birth to flesh, but the Spirit gives birth to spirit (John 3:3, 6)." Thus only Jesus can give birth to our spirit, and we must be born through Him in order to enter into God's kingdom. Are you ready to be born again and transformed by letting Jesus Christ into your larkspur glen?

Jesus spoke to me through this song. I had come to Him long ago but needed to be born again in His love. If you are suffering hardship, loss, or physical or psychiatric illness, don't give up. Jesus wants you to fall in love with Him all over again. Of course you still need to follow your doctors' advice and continue taking any prescribed medications, but you can count on Jesus to restore you physically, mentally, emotionally, and spiritually. He is the Great Physician through His love. He wants to invite you into the larkspur glen of your own soul where you can fall in love with Him all over again and achieve your God-given potential.

Are You a Musician of Silence?

Be still and know that I am God.

Psalm 46:10A

Do you stop and listen to Jesus in the silence of your mind and heart? Do you hear His gentle knock, his gentle voice? Does He walk with you through the garden of your soul?

Let Jesus be your musician of silence. Let Him teach you how to play. You will be able to make beautiful music together with Him.

Musician of Silence
Lyrics and Melody by Diana Wilcox
Musical Arrangement by Bryant Pugh
Produced by Bunny Sigler
©2010 Diana Wilcox

Dr. Diana Wilcox

She sits in her halo
Beneath the stained glass.
My neighbor I know,
But who has she asked
To call on me
In my humble abode?
Is God Himself
Feeling my load?
Chorus:
Musician of silence
Musician of grace
Thunder is written
All over your face.
Saint like an angel
Your harp is so loud.
You must be wrapped in
God's heavenly shroud.
Concealing a Book
That glistens of gold
She prays to heaven
My story's all told.
Balancing love
So pale
And so frail, seventy years
Of God's Holy Grail.
Chorus:

Thank God in Advance

Musician of silence
Musician of grace
Thunder is written
All over your face.
Saint like an angel
Your harp is so loud.
You must be wrapped in
God's heavenly shroud.
God grant her peace
And make her strong
For in Your eyes is where
She belongs.
Raise her high
And give her sight.
Poise her for
This evening's flight.
Cast her over
This great nation
And let her pray
For all your creation.
And with each breath's deep release,
let her pray a song of peace.
Chorus:
Musician of silence
Musician of grace
Thunder is written

Dr. Diana Wilcox

All over your face.
Saint like an angel
Your harp is so loud.
You must be wrapped in
God's heavenly shroud.
Somehow I know
She is praying for me
For God you've come
To set me free.
Lord, when she comes to
Take her last flight
Accept her so quickly
Accept her so tight
Let her not feel
One ounce of pain
For she has brought You
To me again.
Chorus:
Musician of silence
Musician of grace
Thunder is written
All over your face.
Saint like an angel
Your harp is so loud.
You must be wrapped in
God's heavenly shroud.

Thank God in Advance

The song "Musician of Silence" was written for my dear friend Charlotte, an older lady who lived next door to me during the time that I lived with my first husband. She knew some of the challenges I was facing, and she was a strong Christian example for me. One night I was passing by my window, and I saw her in her window, long hair flowing, looking over at our house, and I knew she was praying. This is how she looked—like a saintly and thunderously still musician of silence. I shared some of my lyrics with Charlotte, and she told me that if I could write like that it must be hard for me to not have a creative outlet. I am grateful to Charlotte for doing her best to lead me closer to Christ at the time and for encouraging me in my Christian walk during a very dark time in my life.

The song itself was inspired by the French song "Sainte," which was written by Stephane Mallarme (1842-1898). The song says, "Musician of silence, musician of grace, thunder is written all over your face. Saint like an angel your harp is so loud. You must be wrapped in God's heavenly shroud." The irony here is that a musician of silence can play very loudly to God in pure silence. There is great power in prayer, even in silent prayer. "The prayer of a righteous man is powerful and effective" (James 5:16).

The song goes on, "Cast her over this great nation, and let her pray for all your creation. And with each breath's deep release, let her pray a song of peace." This is really what we all need to be doing. We need to pray for our cities, our states, our nation, and the peace of our world. After all this, the song says that, "Somehow I know she is praying for me, for God you've come to set me free." It is amazing how a God that can control the entire universe can also control the details of our lives if we just have faith in Him to do so.

I am very grateful to Charlotte for praying for me and pray only the best for her to have a long, happy, and abundant life. "Lord, when she comes to take her last flight, accept her so quickly. Accept her so tight. Let her not feel one ounce of pain for she has brought you to me again."

Injustice to Sweet Justice

The Lord loves righteousness and justice; the earth is full of his unfailing love.

Psalm 33:5

Sweet Justice
Lyrics and Melody by
Diana Wilcox
Musical Arrangement by
Bryant Pugh
Produced by Bunny Sigler
©2010 *Diana Wilcox*

Injustice
Injustice
There is injustice in my life.
Injustice
Injustice
That only You can set right.
Chorus:
Will You come down
From way on high?

Dr. Diana Wilcox

And set these scales
By Your eye?
Will You come down
From way on high
And set these scales
By Your eye?
If I just seek
I know I'll find
Cause 'til now
I've been so blind.
It's just a walk across the floor.
It's just an op'nin up the door.
Chorus:
And You'll come down
From way on high.
You'll set these scales
By Your eye.
Yes, You'll come down
From way on high
And set these scales
By Your eye.
I go and open up the door
And I'm changed forevermore!
And in sure ain't no surprise!
You've set those scales
— By your eyes!

Chorus:
Yes, You've come down
From way on high
You've set these scales
By your eyes!
Yes, You've come down
From way on high
And set these scales
By Your eyes!
Sweet Justice
Sweet Justice
There is sweet justice
In my life.
Sweet Justice
Sweet Justice
That only You
Could set right.

In a previous chapter, I told you about a song I wrote called "Sweet Justice." I was devastated by the injustice in my life after my divorce. In the song, I pray to God and say, "There is injustice in my life that only you can set right." Then I ask Him, "Will you come down from way on high and set these scales by Your eye?" This song was a great comfort to me. It was actually dictated to me by God, and I just sang it into the tape recorder as He sang it. I really can't take any credit for it. Praise be to God for His great comfort it times of trouble. It was then that I knew I couldn't do anything about the situation myself, except pray for God to set things right in His own way, in his own time.

The song is about having faith in God to set things right in His own way. "Faith is being sure of what we hope for and certain of what we do not see" (Hebrews 11:1). And as the song says, "And it sure ain't no surprise! You've set those scales by your eyes!" Then the song just ends in a savoring of the sweet justice of God in my life, that only He could set right. In my case, the sweet justice was simply to be able to savor the joy of Jesus again in my life and to enjoy my children and the life I have with my new husband and to do my best to spread God's word and win souls for Jesus Christ. I did not write the last verse of the song about "sweet justice" until several years later, but I always remembered God's promise to me that one day the scales of justice would be set by His eye. It was then that I changed the title of the song from "Injustice" to "Sweet Justice."

God is a just and merciful God, but He never promised us that there would at all times be justice for us in this world. Indeed Jesus said, "Remember the words I spoke to you, 'No servant is greater than his master.' If they persecuted me, they will persecute you also" (John 15:20A). God does promise us, however, that in His own way, in His own time, His justice and mercy will prevail, even if that is in heaven or in the second coming. We can all choose whether or not we will serve God, but we cannot choose whether or not we will bow down to Him. There are no atheists in hell. Everyone, whether they go to heaven or to hell, eventually bows down to Jesus Christ. "Before me every knee will bow; by me every tongue will swear (Isaiah 45:23)."

I sang this song for a fellow driving a shuttle bus to the airport who said he was going through a hard time. After I finished the song, he pulled the bus over in the middle of his route, gave me a big hug and told me how much the song blessed him! Thank you Jesus! Thank you God, the Father of all comfort! Thank you for helping this one man with your promise of Sweet Justice!

Green Is My Love Eternal

Here I am! I stand at the door and knock. If anyone hears my voice and opens the door, I will come in and eat with him, and he with me.

Revelation 3:20

Green is My Love
Lyrics and Melody by
Diana Wilcox
Musical Arrangement by
Bryant Pugh
Produced by Bunny Sigler
©2007 Diana Wilcox

Green is my love
Like the forest rare
Warm is my love
Like the sun
Shining fair.
Deep is my love

Dr. Diana Wilcox

Like the roots of the trees
Vast is my love
Like her branches
In the breeze.
Sweet is my love
In lilac flowers' rapture
Glistening is my love
In the dewdrops
They have captured.
Chorus:
Such a joy!
Such a dance!
In this sacred romance.
Turn around!
Make a sound!
Shout for joy!
You have been found!
I wait for you in
The forest green
I wait for you
Can you divine
What I mean?
Look way deep into
My creation.
Tune right in to a
Brand new station.

Thank God in Advance

> Love, Love, Love
> It is in the air
> The kind of love
> When you really care.
> *Chorus:*
> Such a joy!
> Such a dance!
> In this sacred romance.
> Turn around!
> Make a sound!
> Shout for joy!
> You have been found!
> God bless you
> When you read
> My Word
> Upon the flight
> Of a single bird.
> There are many who fly.
> There are many who fall,
> But you will find that my love
> carries them all.

Like "The Larkspur Glen", the song "Green Is My Love" was also written as a celebration of Jesus's love for us. Evidence of God's creation and His love for us is throughout nature. As the song says, "I wait for you in the forest green." We need only to enter the deepest place of our souls and invite Jesus in.

The song speaks of the great joy I have found in knowing Jesus. At the time I wrote this song, my current husband and I were temporarily separated. Thus my time with Jesus became like a sacred romance, for I wanted to be with no one but Him.

The song says, "God bless you when you read my Word upon the flight of a single bird." Too often we, in our modern world, forget to look for God in the nature He created. Nature is evidence of God's great majesty, and we need to respect and conserve our natural world.

The last verse is about all of us who have ups and downs, but especially those of us who have manic and depressive episodes. "There are many who fly. There are many who fall, but you will find that my love carries them all." Jesus has a special grace for those with afflictions and if you search deeply enough you will find that love for yourself. The lyrics for this song were inspired by the German song "Meine Liebe Ist Grun" by Felix Schumann and Johannes Brahms, Op. 63, no. 5.

Prayer for the Tinman

Then your light will break forth like the dawn, and your healing will quickly appear.

Isaiah 58:8A

Prayer for the Tinman
Lyrics and Melody by
Diana Wilcox
Musical Arrangement by
Bryant Pugh
Produced by Bunny Sigler
©2010 Diana Wilcox

You could speak three languages,
But not the language of the heart.
Only wish I quit translatin'
From the very start.
Taught me how to curse in French
Without a comment-allez vous,

Dr. Diana Wilcox

But even that fancy langue Francaise
Couldn't perfume up the truth.
Never heard you sing
"If I only had a heart,"
'stead you banged your fists
against an empty drum
'til our love broke apart.
And now your tryin'
To tell my whole life
With your lies and deceit.
Ain't ever gonna kill me softly
With your songs of conceit.
Chorus:
So there ain't no use sweet-talkin'
Folks on an' on in French
Cause your killin' em
With kindness comes back to
Haunt you inch by inch.
Your smooth teflon reputation
Right here is on the line
Peelin' back like an old fry pan
That's done lost its shine.
And that turnin' up the heat you do
When you got a victim pinned
Won't smelt out a heart o' gold
From that hollow drum o' tin.

Thank God in Advance

> The only one your foolin' child
> Is not a man of steel,
> But a tinman stuck
> In the woods of time
> Because he cannot feel.
> Now one of these days when
> That ol' tinman's been
> through some pain,
> He'll drink a cup o' kindness
> Anoint him just like rain!
> And on that day the squeaky wheel
> Will finally get some grease,
> And that's the day the tinman will
> Walk through these woods in peace.

I wrote this song about the breakup with my first husband. The "tinman" is "stuck in the woods of time." He has been traumatized and numbed by his own past. This song was very healing to me in venting my anger at one time, but it certainly is no longer reflective of the way I feel now. I must confess that I did not have forgiveness in my heart when I wrote the first few verses of this song. It was not until a year later that I found forgiveness in my heart and completed the song.

The last two verses of the song say, " Now one of these days when that ol' tinman's been through some pain, he'll drink a cup o' kindness, anoint him just like rain, and on that day the squeaky wheel will finally get some grease, and that's the day the tinman will walk through these woods in peace." The song offers hope that one day "the tinman" will repent to God, drink a cup of God's kindness, become anointed, and finally find peace with God. I wish only blessings for my first husband. I am very grateful to him for how well he has taken care of my first two children. He has been a blessing to them. Since this song was recorded, I have apologized to him for the song and told him that I have long since forgiven him as well.

It's Our Time

Let the little children come to me and do not hinder them, for the kingdom of God belongs to such as these.

Luke 18:16

It's Our Time
Lyrics and Melody by Diana Wilcox
Musical Arrangement by Bryant Pugh
Produced by Bunny Sigler
©2010 Diana Wilcox

It's our time, our time
to laugh and sing.
It's our time, let's see
what we can bring.
Somewhere past the mountains
Somewhere past the pain
Is a time that you and I
Have so much more to gain.

Dr. Diana Wilcox

> It's our time, our time to be strong.
> Our time to see that you and I
> Really do belong.
> We listen to our feelings.
> We talk with one another
> Cause our time kids, we all know,
> We're sisters and we're brothers.
> It's our time, our time
> to laugh and sing.
> It's our time, what happy
> hearts we'll bring.

This song was actually written for a children's television program that I was hoping to produce at one time. Fred Rogers, who produced *Mr. Rogers' Neighborhood* as an ordained Presbyterian minister, had always been a hero of mine since childhood. At one time, I was hoping to produce a similar program called *It's Our Time* or *Dr. Heaven's Home*. I actually produced a pilot for the program and shopped it around, but was told that it needed to be animated.

So often children don't have their own time with parents, who are so busy these days working, making dinner, paying bills, and just preoccupied with life. The song "It's Our Time" emphasizes that we need to have a special time with our children, giving them our full attention, by reading them a book, coloring, playing with toys, or just interacting in some special way.

Angels Fly through Heaven

For he will command his angels concerning you to guard you in all your ways

Psalm 91:11

Angels Fly Through Heaven
Lyrics and Melody by Diana Wilcox
Musical Arrangement by Bryant Pugh
Produced by Bunny Sigler
©2010 Diana Wilcox

Angels fly through heaven
Somewhere way up there.
They come down to Earth to see us
Because they really care.
About all the special children
Living here and there,
In each and every country
Their each and every hair.
It's all the special children

Dr. Diana Wilcox

> That really need our love
> Because all of us are special
> To someone up above.
> Angels fly through heaven
> Somewhere way up there.
> They come down to Earth to see us
> Because they really care.
> Because they really care.
> Because they really care.

This is a children's song about the comfort of angels visiting us from heaven. It reminds me of the vision I had of my father visiting me from heaven that I described in a previous chapter. Children especially need the comfort of Jesus and his angels and that includes children of every country. The song sings of God's great love for all His children, "in each and every country, their each and every hair."

PART THREE: FREE AT LAST
God Uses Broken Pieces— Come Broken

God wants you just as you are. You don't have to be "cleaned up" to come before God. Of course there is a time to repent of your sins, but first it is important to just come before God and know that He loves you just the way you are. Of course, as your friend, He wants good things for you and wants you to improve, but only in His time.

In fact, many people don't truly come into a deeper relationship with Christ until they are broken in one way or another by the ravages of this world. You may feel that you are not good enough to come before God or that there is no way He could forgive you. None of us are worthy. As Paul says, "there is no one righteous, not even one" (Romans 3:10).

However, you are His precious child. You are His handiwork, and He made you exactly the way you are. As Psalm 34:18 says, "The Lord is close to the brokenhearted." It doesn't matter who you are or what sins you've committed. As one of our pastors sums it up, "The ground is level at the foot of the cross."

Before Jesus fed the 5,000 with two fish and five loaves, He first broke the fish and the loaves. Precisely "looking up to heaven, he gave thanks and broke them (Luke 9:16)." After the meal, He had His disciples gather up all the broken pieces of fish and bread so that none would be wasted. The Lord can do the same in your life. We need to give all we have to Him, meager as it is, and allow Him to give thanks to God and to "break us." By this I mean that we need to come broken. We need to admit that we are broken in His presence and that we are sinners in need of a savior. It is as simple as that. If you give all you have to Jesus and hold nothing back, He will do nothing short of a miracle in your life. Just as He had the disciples gather the remnants of the fish and loaves, He will gather up the remnants of your life so that nothing will be wasted. Come broken and expect a miracle. As the

Lord says in Isaiah 61:7, "Instead of their shame, my people will receive a double portion."

Part of coming broken to the cross is having faith in Jesus. There are no atheists in hell. "It is written: 'As surely as I live,' says the Lord, 'every knee will bow before me; every tongue will confess to God (Romans 14:11)." This means that even those who are atheists here on earth will bow before God before they go to hell. You don't have to have a tremendous amount of faith to come to the cross or to bear fruit in God's name. Jesus said in Matthew 17:20, "I tell you the truth, if you have faith small as a mustard seed, you can say to the mountain, 'Move from here to there' and it will move. Nothing will be impossible for you."

Pray with me: Lord, Let me come to you broken, just the way I am. You made me exactly the way I am, and I know you are close to the brokenhearted. Teach me to give all that I have to you. Use me to do your will. Please gather up the remnants of my life and create a new life for me so that nothing will be wasted. Grant me a double portion for my past shame. Increase my faith in you each day. Help me to accept Jesus into my heart and to make Him the savior of my life. In Jesus's name, Amen.

Praise God the Father of All Comfort

Praise be to the God and Father of our Lord Jesus Christ, the Father of compassion and the God of all comfort, who comforts us in all our troubles, so that we can comfort those in any trouble with the comfort we ourselves have received from God.

2 Corinthians 1: 3-4

Praise God for comforting you, even if you don't feel it now. Praise Him in advance for His comfort and compassion. Have faith, and you will begin to feel His comfort enveloping you. One of the best ways to feel God's comfort is to turn it around and comfort someone else. You'll realize that you have more strength than you thought you had. Nothing is too great or too small for God. You may feel that your burdens are too big. Nothing is too great for God to handle. You may feel that your burdens are so small in the scope of things that they don't matter to God. This is not true. God cares about every burden you have. He counts every tear you shed. "Record my lament; list my tears on your scroll— are they not in your record? (Psalm 56:8)."

Again, take heart and praise God for his comfort. These days we are tricked into thinking that we can get real comfort from other things in this world. The real comfort, however, comes from reading your Bible and spending time in prayer with Jesus. If you realized how much comfort and compassion Jesus would show you in your life, would you be willing to spend more time with Him?

Pray with me: Lord I ask you to help me to make more time for you in my life. Let me spend more time reading my Bible and praying to you so that I may receive your deep comfort and compassion. Help me to share that comfort and compassion with others in any trouble they may have. I have faith that I will begin to feel your comfort enveloping me in my own affliction. In Jesus's name, Amen.

Fall In Love with Jesus

Falling in love with Jesus is the most powerful thing you can do in your healing. It is following the first of the two greatest commandments: "Love the Lord your God with all your heart and with all your soul and with all your mind and with all your strength (Mark 12:30)." Jesus is the Son of God. He is God made flesh.

As Jesus says, "Greater love has no one than this, that he lay down his life for his friends (John 15:13)." Jesus loved us so much that He laid down his life that our sins might be forgiven and that we might have eternal life. It wasn't the nails that held Him to the cross. He could have called down a legion of angels to rescue Him, but He chose to die for our sins. There on the cross, like on a cosmic radio station, He tuned in to every sin that all humanity for all eternity would ever commit and became that sin. As a perfect sacrifice, free of all sin Himself, He cancelled our sins for all eternity so that we may appear before God the Father washed clean in His blood. "I tell you the truth; no one can see the kingdom of God unless he is born again" (John 3:3).

God sent Jesus, because it was the only way that we humans would begin to understand His great love for us. "For God so loved the world that He gave His one and only Son, that whoever believes in Him shall not perish but have eternal life" (John 3:16). These are all compelling reasons to fall in love with God and Jesus.

Jesus loves you exactly the way you are and has great plans for you. You are precious to Him. You may have had or may still have people in your life who do not value you. It may be time for you to make a new and different set of friends. Know that you are royalty to God and that you have God's abundant favor! You need to allow yourself to believe in God's promises. Don't let other people's expectations of you hold you back! You need to allow yourself to believe in Jesus. If you believe in Jesus, and do not deny His name, He will believe in you in this life and on the day of your judgment. Allow Him the privilege of being there to put his arm around you when you are asked to account for your life by God the Father. Allow Him to be there to say, "Don't worry Dad, this one is mine, he belongs to me" or "she belongs to me." Fall in love with Jesus. "Give thanks to the Lord, for his love endures forever (2 Chronicles 20:21)."

Be faithful to Jesus and remain in the Spirit. Don't make the mistake I did and dabble in other religions, trying to be diplomatic, or, as some people do, trying to make things more interesting. Just as a husband does not want his wife to date other men, Jesus does not want His bride to stray into other religions. It's as simple as that. This is not so much for His sake, but for our own. There are consequences for not following Jesus's direction. As Jesus said, "I am the way and the truth and the life. No one comes to the Father except through me (John 14:6)." Do you honestly love only Jesus? Do you believe Him when He says that no one comes to the Father except through Him? Are you toying with other religions? As Paul writes, "Love must be sincere (Romans 12:9)."

Pray with me: Dear Jesus, please help me to fall in love with you and only you. Help me to fully realize how much you love me and help me to start becoming a reflection of that love. Help me to put aside any other religions or distractions that have pulled me away from you, Jesus. Forgive me of my sins and cleanse me of my impurities. Help me to have a loyal and sincere love for you and you alone. Help me to fall more deeply in love with you every day. In Jesus's name, Amen.

Live to Please God

Too many of us live to please other people. I grew up living to please my mother. Sadly, I did not learn the value of just saying no to people until I became older. Then it was very challenging for me to learn how to do this. To this day there are people who have cast me aside because of my psychiatric label, and it hurts not to have their approval.

However I do not need the approval of man, but the approval of God. Another thing that held me back from singing in public in the past is that I occasionally have to look at the words to my songs while I sing. However I have decided that that is okay. I am different, and I don't have to follow a prescribed format for performing my songs. In the future when I sing in public, I am going to focus less on myself and others, and more on God and ministering to his children.

What about you? Are you living your life to fulfill a label or other people's expectations of you?

Pray with me: In the name of Jesus, I hereby come against the stigma of any label or negative expectation that has been placed on me by others that is holding me back from receiving my God-given potential. Lord, let me seek your approval alone and not man's approval. Let everything I do be for the glory of God. In Jesus's name, Amen.

Take Care of Jesus's Bride

Jesus loves the church like a groom loves his bride. Taking care of Jesus's bride, including yourself, involves following the second commandment "Love your neighbor as yourself" (Mark 12:31). Do you love yourself? Do you love your neighbor? Do you fully appreciate your church community? Do you pray for your pastors and ministry staff? Do you think of yourself and your fellow believers as part of Jesus's bride? You are special to Jesus. "Fear not, for I have redeemed you; I have summoned you by name; you are mine (Isaiah 43:1)." As Jesus said, "You did not choose me, but I chose you and appointed you to go and bear fruit—fruit that will last. Then the Father will give you whatever you ask in my name (John 15:16)."

Jesus loves you so much that He wants you to take care of yourself. He has summoned you by name and appointed you to do great things! You may think that Jesus has the wrong person. You may be thinking that you are not worthy or capable or educated enough to do great things, but that is wrong. You are looking at yourself through the eyes of the world. Look at yourself through Jesus's eyes and you will see someone very different. Can you see yourself with eyes of compassion? Can you have compassion for the little child that you once were? That is how Jesus still sees you—as His child.

Jesus's disciples were not the most educated people around, but Jesus did not choose them as the world would have chosen them. He chose eleven loyal disciples who would spread his Word throughout the world after His death and resurrection. He has also chosen you to do the same.

Jesus has appointed you to bear fruit—to do a mission in this world. Will you be able to add souls to your name? Will you be able to encourage others? Will you be able to be of service in the church? Ask Jesus for guidance and vision as you draw closer to Him. You are His. God had this purpose for you before He created the universe so have faith. "You are a chosen people, a royal priesthood (1 Peter 2:9)."

Pray with me: Lord, allow me to prepare myself for you as a bride prepares herself for her groom on her wedding day! Teach me how to truly take care of

Thank God in Advance

myself and love myself. Teach me to realize that you have summoned me by name and appointed me to bear fruit for you. Teach me to love others more and to pray for my church and my pastors. Please guide me and give me vision as to your purpose for me in my life. In Jesus's name, Amen.

Walk the Walk–Practice Self-Discipline

When you take care of yourself as Jesus's bride you are responsible to love yourself. However, you are also responsible to have self-discipline. In other words, you must walk the walk and dedicate all arenas of your life to Jesus. If you are expecting Jesus to change your life, don't hold back. What if the boy with the two fish and five loaves had kept half of it for himself? Would Jesus still have performed a miracle and fed the 5,000 with what he had to give Him? Probably not! You see the boy had a child's faith in Jesus and gave all that he had! This is what you must do with your life too. If you are engaging in sinful behavior against God you need to repent and stop it for your own sake! God cannot do a miracle in your life unless you come to Him fully.

> Clothe yourselves with the Lord Jesus Christ, and do not think about how to gratify the desires of the sinful nature.
>
> Romans 13:14

> The acts of the sinful nature are obvious: sexual immorality, impurity, and debauchery, idolatry and witchcraft; hatred, discord, jealousy, fits of rage, selfish ambition, dissensions, factions and envy; drunkenness, orgies, and the like. I warn you, as I did before, that those who live like this will not inherit the kingdom of God.
>
> Galatians 5:19-21

What parts of your life are you holding back from Jesus? Is it a behavioral addiction to anger or to gambling or to food? Is it procrastination about reading your Bible and fulfilling God's plan in your life? Is it your sex life? Are you having sex outside of marriage? God has very clear guidelines on sexual immorality.

> Flee from sexual immorality. All other sins a man commits are outside his body, but he who sins sexually sins against his

> own body. Do you not know that your body is a temple of the Holy Spirit, who is in you, whom you have received from God? You are not your own; you were bought at a price. Therefore honor God with your body.
>
> 1 Corinthians 6:18-20

Apart from the sanctity of marriage, only Jesus can provide the love many people mistakenly look for in a sexual relationship. Your body is God's temple and should be treated as such. You are valuable to God.

If you are a young woman or have a young daughter coming of age I would suggest reading *Every Young Woman's Battle: Guarding Your Mind, Heart, and Body in a Sex-Saturated World* by Shannon Ethridge. According the Bible, God views premarital sex as a sin. It can also be very distracting from your studies, your vocation, and from understanding God's overall vision for your life. It makes breakups a lot harder to take. Some men don't respect women after they have had sex with them unless they have married them. Then there are some men who see no reason to get married to become more emotionally intimate in the relationship since they are already getting what they think they want. Plus, no matter how careful you are using birth control, there's always the possibility of an accident. Waiting around for your period to start, worrying that you may be pregnant, can be very scary.

You need to realize and believe that you are a precious child of God and that your body is a sacred temple. Any man who wants to have sex with you should be man enough to wait until you say it is the right time and to marry you first among your family and friends. If you pray for wisdom, God will grant it to you just like He did King Solomon. The fruit of the Spirit when Jesus dwells in your heart is "joy, peace, patience, kindness, goodness, faithfulness, gentleness, and self-control. Against such things there is no law (Galatians 5:22-23)."

It is not enough to just call on the name of Jesus if you do not also believe in Him and try to follow His will. Jesus said, "Many will say to me on that day, 'Lord Lord, did we not prophesy in your name, and in your name drive out demons and perform many miracles?' Then I will tell them plainly, 'I never knew you. Away with me, you evil doers!' (Matthew 7:22-23)." It is important to read the Bible and draw closer to God so that you will know what God's will is for you!

Thank God in Advance

Part of having self-discipline means taking care of God's temple, your physical body. This means faithfully taking any medication that your physician has prescribed for you. It is also important to get good nutrition, exercise, sleep, rest, and plenty of sunshine. I am not a nutritionist, but I can heartily recommend both the Zone Diet by Dr. Barry Sears and the Maker's Diet by Jason Rubin. It is especially important if you have a psychiatric illness to have good nutrition with moderate amounts of protein, lot of fruits and vegetables, very little caffeine, sugars and starches, and plenty of water, all in order to keep your mood stable.

Pray with me: Dear God, help me to dedicate all arenas of my life to you. You are all-knowing and all-powerful. I do not want to hold back anything from you. Teach me to give all I have to you. Help me to give up any parts of my life that I have been holding back from you, Lord. In the name of Jesus, I hereby break the bonds of addiction, sin, and the misuse of the temple you have given me. Help me to take care of this physical body you have given me so that I may use it to your glory. In Jesus's name, Amen.

Forgive as He Forgave You

Jesus set the ultimate example of forgiveness when He was dying on the cross and said, "Forgive them Father for they know not what they do." Indeed, unless we are led by the Holy Spirit, we are ignorant, blind, and lost and know not what we do. Even then we are all sinners and need God's constant guidance. Don't hold grudges against those who have hurt you. Holding grudges hurts you more than them. It embitters your heart and keeps God from fully being able to forgive you of your sins.

Once we repent of our sins, God also wants us to forgive ourselves. An important point that Anne Graham Lotz makes is that when we do not forgive ourselves we are saying that we have higher standards than God, who forgives us fully and completely. Forgiving yourself is not an easy task. Satan wants to press us down by reminding us of our sins. Satan wants to judge and condemn us, but "there is now no condemnation for those who are in Christ Jesus (Romans 8:1)." In Paul's words, "Forgetting what is behind and straining toward what is ahead, I press on toward the goal to win the prize for which God has called me heavenward in Christ Jesus (Philippians 3:13-14)."

Keep in mind that there will be some people who you may share your story with who may judge and condemn you. These people may even call themselves Christians. Ask God to bless and forgive them for they know not what they do. You will come out of the fire like Shadrach, Meshach and Abednego did, without a smell of smoke, for Jesus walks with you (see Daniel 3:27). It is hard to forgive yourself though, when you know that others you used to look up to condemn you. This is when you have to stop relying on others for validation, and rely on the Lord. The more practice you have at this the easier it becomes.

Forgiving yourself is truly an act of humility, because it is putting God above yourself and your sin. When you magnify your sin and dwell on it in guilt as Satan would have you do, you are actually making an idol out of your sin. You need to be dwelling on God. He should be on the throne of your soul and your mind, and not your worry over your past sins. Humble yourself, repent, and do your best to sin no more.

It is hard to forgive yourself unless you know how to forgive others and vice-versa. Practice at one helps with being able to do the other. When you don't forgive yourself, you are not accepting God's greatest gift to us. God sent His Son, Jesus, to die on the cross for us so that our sins would be forgiven. Is Jesus's death on the cross to forgive your sins not enough for you? Are you expecting something more from Him? What more could He have done for you? Think about this and surely you will come around to forgiving yourself.

The more sins that Jesus has forgiven us the more grateful we are to Him for washing us as white as snow. In Luke, Jesus tells the story of two men, one who owes a moneylender 500 denarii and one who owes him 50 denarii. "Neither of them had the money to pay him back so he cancelled the debts of both. Now which of them will love him more? (Luke 7:41-42)." Of course the man who had the biggest debt will love the money lender more. By dying for our sins, Jesus has cancelled *all* of our debts! If you are overburdened by your sins and you repent, rest assured that your love for Jesus will, in turn, be stronger than if you had taken a shorter journey to Jesus.

Let us pray: Dear Lord, You forgive us of our sins even when we don't deserve your forgiveness. Help us learn to forgive ourselves. We realize that the enemy wants us to magnify our sins rather than to magnify You. Lord, help us to understand that there is no condemnation for those who are now in Jesus Christ. Teach us to forgive others and to let go of grudges and bitter feelings. Let us appreciate how your Son's dying on the cross cancelled all our debts and all the debts of humanity. In Jesus's name, Amen.

Bless Your Abusers

"Bless those who persecute you; bless and do not curse. Rejoice with those who rejoice; mourn with those who mourn (Romans 12:15)." We are to bless our abusers and not curse them. This of course does not mean that you have to keep taking the abuse. God in no way wants you to be harmed. However, once you are out of harm's way, God wants you to pray for and bless those who persecute you. Pray that all the wonderful things you pray happen to you will also happen to them. Believe it or not this will ease your heart and take the bitterness out of your spirit. Even more challenging, rejoice when your abuser rejoices and mourn when your abuser mourns.

Remember that the Lord will work out justice in his own way in his own time. "Do not repay anyone evil for evil... Do not take revenge (Romans 12:17, 19)." Instead, be kind to your abuser, and, in doing so, you will cause him to repent. Abraham Lincoln was once chastised for being so courteous to the world leaders many considered his enemies. When asked, "Why do you treat them like friends?", he responded, "If I make them my friends, have I not lost them as my enemies?"

Pray with me: Dear Lord, Like Abraham Lincoln, help me turn my enemies into friends. Teach me to pray for my enemies and for those who persecute me. Teach me to mourn when they mourn and rejoice when they rejoice. Give me a new heart of understanding and compassion for them. In Jesus's name, Amen.

Sing a Song of Praise and Joy

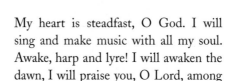

> My heart is steadfast, O God. I will sing and make music with all my soul. Awake, harp and lyre! I will awaken the dawn, I will praise you, O Lord, among the nations, I will sing of you among the peoples.
>
> Psalm 108:1-3

Praise the Lord for who He is. Praise Him for His majesty and for His humanity. Praise Him for all the blessings in your life. Start each prayer with praise for all He has done, is doing, and is about to do for you. You will find that the Lord will give you "a crown of beauty instead of ashes, the oil of gladness instead of mourning, and a garment of praise instead of a spirit of despair" (Isaiah 61:1). Remember that you have a personal relationship with God, and, that like anyone else, God appreciates a compliment or two, especially before being given a "honey-do" list!

Pray with me: Dear God, I want to learn to praise you more and more each day. You are all-knowing and all-powerful, Creator of heaven and earth, and of all the universe. I humbly acknowledge You as the Lord of my life. Teach me to sing a joyful song of praise in my heart to you each day! In Jesus's name, Amen

Humbly Serve Others

"Humble yourselves, therefore under God's mighty hand, that He may lift you up in due time" (1 Peter 5:6). Humbling yourself is an automatic way to become less self-absorbed. When we are self-absorbed we are miserable. We have put ourselves on the throne of our souls instead of God. I have learned the hard way that this is no way to live.

I used to know an amazing 98-year-old African American man with blue eyes who walked with his cane like a king. Everyone called him King. (His identity has been disguised for confidentiality). He only talked when people asked him to share a word, and when he did, he had a lot of wisdom in all those years of living. Once I asked him what advice he would give the President of the United States if he were here today listening to him. He sat back and thought a minute, and several 80-year-old ladies who were there sat on the edge of their seats waiting to hear what this 98-year-old man would say. King said, "I would tell the president—*Never* pass up a chance to humble yourself! Great nations have fallen due to a lack of humility!"

And all were silent there for a while. King had spoken a word that every president and that all of us should hear. Why is humility so important? How could a lack of humility cause an entire nation to crumble? Well, it's starting to happen now, isn't it? The world tells us to put ourselves first, to look out for number one. When we erect an idol to ourselves we are committing idolatry before God and breaking one of the Ten Commandments. Again, idolizing ourselves and our abilities and accomplishments only makes us miserable. We are getting caught up in what the world says to do. We are investing in something that is temporary and ever changing and prone to error. As it says in Proverbs 16:18, "Pride goes before destruction, a haughty spirit before a fall."

The best way to show God that you are ready to be lifted up to the next level is to become a servant to others. As Jesus said,

> Instead, whoever wants to become great among you must be your servant, and

> whoever wants to be first must be your slave—just as the Son of Man did not come to be served, but to serve, and to give his life as a ransom for many.
>
> Matthew 20:26-28

Thus Jesus was the perfect example of serving others, even to the point of death on a cross to save us from our sins. Demonstrating this humility, He washed the feet of His disciples (John 13). He showed us how we ought to treat each other, as servants to each other. "Do nothing out of selfish ambition or vain conceit, but in humility consider others better than ourselves" (Philippians 2:3).

Part of humbly serving others is giving God the glory for the things you accomplish.

In all things you do, give God the glory. For if you give God the glory then you put Him rightly on the throne of your soul. "For it is by grace you have been saved, through faith—and this not from yourselves, it is the gift of God—not by works, so that no one can boast" (Ephesians 2:8).

As individuals we need to humble ourselves before God and to ask Him to use us as His servants. Then we will find that He lifts us up to new heights beyond which we could have never attained on our own. As Queen said, we should never pass up a chance to humble ourselves.

Our nation was built upon Christian values and principles. As a nation we need to be proud of our heritage but also need to humble ourselves before God. We need to give God the glory for our strengths and accomplishments rather than idolizing ourselves. We need to be a servant and helpmate to other nations in times of trouble and in times of peace. Then God will lift us up as a nation for his glory. With a good dose of humility, our nation will be stronger than ever.

Pray with me: Dear God, Teach me to be your humble servant and a servant to those around me. Help me to not do things out of vain ambition, but out of love for You and for your children. Help me to be an example of how Americans need to be, humble helpmates to other nations in times of trouble and in times of peace. For you have said that those who put themselves last will be first. In Jesus's name, Amen.

Put on the Armor of God

You can count on the fact that as a Christian the enemy will attack you. The more you want to get close to Jesus the more you are a threat to the enemy. The more you spread Jesus's word, the more the enemy will try to attack you. Many people make the false assumption that once they become a Christian their troubles will cease. This is not true. First, there is the trouble that comes simply from living in a fallen world. Second, there is the additional persecution that can come from being a Christian. Jesus warned us of this. "No servant is greater than his master. If they persecuted me, they will persecute you also" (John 16:20).

You need to prepare for battle not against people, but against principalities of spiritual darkness; "For our struggle is not against flesh and blood, but against the rulers, against the authorities, against the powers of this dark world and against the spiritual forces of evil in the heavenly realms" (Ephesians 6:12). If you are suffering from past abuse or trauma or from having lived a sinful life up to this point, you need to "put on the full armor of God so that you can take your stand against the devil's schemes... stand firm then, with the belt of truth buckled around your waist, with the breastplate of righteousness in place, and with your feet fitted with the readiness that comes from the gospel of peace. In addition to all this, take up the shield of faith, with which you can extinguish all the flaming arrows of the evil one. Take the helmet of salvation, and the sword of the Spirit, which is the word of God" (Ephesians 6:10-17).

Pray with me: Dear God, Thank you for giving me armor to defend against the enemy. Help me to put on that armor every day, filling me with faith, and arming me with your precious Word. Create a hedge around me and my loved ones on all sides so that no weapon forged against us will proper. Surround us with your angels of protection. In Jesus's name, Amen.

Overcome Fears

"Fan the gift of God which is in you, through the laying on of hands. For God did not give us a spirit of timidity, but a spirit of power, of love and of self-discipline" (2 Timothy 1:6-7).

God has given you a great gift. That gift is inside of you. Is fear keeping you from opening the gift that God has given you? Where is that fear coming from? It's coming from the enemy. If you have a positive reverential fear of God, that fear needs to override any fear you have of people or things. God wants you to use the gifts He has given you. He wants you to focus on pleasing Him rather than on pleasing other people or on avoiding discomfort. As it says in Proverbs 22:4, "Humility and the fear of the Lord bring wealth and honor and life."

Joshua had to face his fears when he led the Israelites out of the wilderness into the Promised Land. They had been wandering around in the wilderness for forty years! God encouraged him, "Be strong and courageous because you will lead these people to inherit the land I swore to their forefathers to give them (Joshua 1:5)." As Christians we need to be strong and courageous because we are leading others by our example into the kingdom of God that Jesus has promised to us. What is your wilderness? What is your comfort zone? God is ready for you to move up to the next level!

God has a gift he wants you to inherit that lies beyond the wilderness! He exhorts you to be strong and courageous so that you can share your gift with others in Christ Jesus. "Be strong and courageous. Do not be terrified; do not be discouraged, for the Lord your God will be with you wherever you go (Joshua 1:9)." This is important. God promises to be with us wherever we go. He is always with us.

Have you been staying in the comfort zone and just wandering around in the wilderness of your soul due to fear? Are you letting fear shape your destiny? It's time to "step up to the plate!" This is a line I used in the song "Thank God In Advance." Now I realize that even though I thought I wrote this song solely about my son overcoming his autism and stepping into his future, I also wrote it about me overcoming my autism and stepping into my future! In writing this book, I am also marketing my songs and leaving the wilderness of my old life behind for the Promised Land of Jesus Christ! I have finally decided to use and share the gift that God has given me!

You can do the same thing with your gift. You may not know what it is yet, but believe me, it's there. Of course, the enemy will bring on fear whenever you do something new, but as John Wayne said, "Courage is feeling the fear but saddling up anyway." You can do it, and you can thank God in advance for all the wonderful blessings that you are going to have.

Pray with me: Dear God, Thank you for your encouragement to help me step out of my comfort zone to a new level of victory in You. Let my positive reverential fear of you override any fear I have of people, things, or new situations. I know you want me to open the gift you have given me in my life. Teach me to stop wandering around in the wilderness of my soul, and instead to embark on a new adventure in You. As Joel Osteen puts it, before I will see my victory manifest on the outside, I need to stir up my faith in You on the inside. Lord, help me focus on that faith in You, instead of on the circumstances of life that surround me. Help me "step out of the boat" and walk with Jesus on the water - focusing on Jesus, rather than the waves crashing around me. For when Peter cried out for Jesus as he became overwhelmed, Jesus immediately reached out his hand and caught him. "You of little faith," he said, "why did you doubt?" (Matthew 14:31b) Help my faith to grow Lord so that I may overcome my fears and do great and mighty things in your name. In Jesus's name, Amen.

Develop Your Spiritual Gifts

> For in him you have been enriched in every way – in all your speaking and in all your knowledge – because our testimony about Christ was confirmed in you. Therefore you do not lack any spiritual gift.
>
> 1 Corinthians 1:5-7

This is addressed to all those who call on the name of the Lord Jesus Christ. This is very exciting! It is a promise from God that in every way we have been enriched through Jesus Christ—in all our speaking and all our knowledge, because of our testimony in Jesus. It is a good idea to start your ministry with your testimony.

As you mature as a Christian, you will no longer be satisfied with simply learning about Jesus. You will want to find a way to share the good news with others in some way. You will still want to follow those who minister to you, but you will also want to begin to minister to others. There are many ways to do this. Your spiritual gift may be service to others. It may be encouragement. It may be knowledge. It may simply be a smile. Ask God to reveal to you your spiritual gifts. Have faith and confidence that God will help you develop your spiritual gifts.

> If a man's gift is prophesying, let him use it in proportion to his faith, if it is serving, let him serve; if it is teaching, let him teach; if it is encouraging, let him encourage; if it is contributing to the needs of others, let him give generously; if it is leadership, let him govern diligently; if it is showing mercy, let him do it cheerfully.
>
> Romans 12:6a-8

Study the Bible

If you want to be able to defend yourself against the enemy, you need to know the Word of God. If you want to truly fall in love with Jesus, you need to know the Word of God.

The Bible is a love letter to you from God. If you had a true love who had written you a letter, you would want to read the letter wouldn't you? You wouldn't just leave it unopened gathering dust somewhere would you? Yet, so often that is what we do with our Bibles. The love letter was written for our benefit, so that we could learn how to live a better, fuller, more satisfying life, and to one day have eternal life in Christ Jesus.

By far the most ingenious method of Bible study I have encountered is that developed and taught by Anne Graham Lotz. This particular method makes the words of the Bible jump off the page—full of personal meaning for the reader. I strongly recommend that you use this method in your own Bible study. The procedure has five steps.

The first step is to read God's Word in a designated passage of scripture. The second step is to make a verse-by-verse list of the facts in the passage you just read. Here Lotz suggests you don't paraphrase but use the actual words from the scripture itself. The third step is to list the spiritual lessons learned from each verse of the scripture. The fourth step is to take each lesson from step three and put it in the form of a personal question for yourself. Then the fifth and final step is called Live in Response. In this step you decide exactly how you are going to respond to what God is saying to you through the passage.

As an example, see Revelation 1:15:

Step 1: Read the Passage

His feet were like bronze glowing in a furnace and his voice was like the sound of rushing waters.

Step 2: What does the passage say?

Jesus's feet were like bronze in a furnace and his voice is like rushing waters.

Step 3: *What does the passage mean? What is the lesson?*
Jesus's feet are able to withstand the heat of a furnace of suffering and his voice is powerful like rushing waters.

Step 4: *Question*
Do I recognize how much Jesus can identify with my suffering and how powerful he is to help relieve that suffering?

Step 5: *Live in Response*
Lord let me understand the extent to which you can understand my suffering and how powerful you are to relieve my suffering and to enable me as I learn to imitate you.

Try this method on your own with your favorite passages of scripture and watch the words jump off the page for you!

Let us pray: Dear Lord, You and your Son, Jesus Christ are revealed to us through your holy Word. Thank you for giving the Bible to me and for making it available to me to read. Help me to read and study it more and more every day so that I may come to know you and your Son, Jesus, more and more as the days go by. Reveal to me the depths of wisdom within your scripture and most importantly help me to develop a closer relationship with You so that I may share that relationship with others.

Pray and Journal Daily

Daily prayer is invaluable. It is especially helpful if you spend a regular time with Jesus and write your prayers down in a journal each day. Morning is an especially good time because it helps you to prepare for the day. You will be able to see with your own eyes how God has answered your prayers and this will increase your faith to do new and better things for Jesus Christ. Below are excerpts from my prayer journal and excerpts from my own work in the Bible Study workbook called *The Vision of His Glory* by Anne Graham Lotz. The excerpts map out how attending a Just Give Me Jesus conference by Lotz catapulted me into a closer relationship with Jesus and into an exciting new vision for my life. The excerpts not only chronicle how this book was written, but also how I went from being too shy and overburdened to sing the songs on my CD to being so on fire for Jesus that I'm excited about singing my songs! (Note that for the sake of space, I have sometimes left out Lotz's Step Two in my journal).

Pray with me: Dear Lord, like the song, What A Friend We Have in Jesus, says, "Oh what peace we often forfeit, oh what needless pain we bear, all because we do not carry everything to God in prayer." You want us to pray to and worship you not because You need our worship, but because you care about us and you know that it is only by prayer and worshiping you that we will have victory in our lives today and for all eternity. Worship is for our own good. Teach me to do as the song says and to simply carry everything to You in prayer. You are God and all things are possible with You. In Jesus's name, Amen.

PART FOUR: JOURNAL AND WORKBOOK EXCERPTS

9-13-09

Dear God,

Thanks for letting me attend the Just Give Me Jesus Conference given by Anne Graham Lotz last weekend. It was very helpful in giving me a new method of studying the Bible verse by verse. Romans 12:1 says to "offer your body as a living sacrifice holy and pleasing to God as an act of worship." I need to serve God in my actions more as a living sacrifice and an act of worship. Verse 2 says, "Do not conform any longer to the pattern of this world, but be transformed by the renewing of your mind. Then you will be able to test and approve what

God's will is—his good and perfect will." Thus I need to be less concerned about the world's expectations of me. Instead, I need to be transformed by Christ's renewal of my mind by spending more time with You and in Your Word. This way the Bible promises that I can have a better perspective on what Your will is for me in my life.

Love, Diana

Luke 9:10-17

What does the passage say?

10. The apostles reported to Jesus and He took them with Him, withdrawing to be alone.
11. The crowds followed them. Jesus welcomed them, spoke about God, and healed people.
12. The disciples told Jesus to send the crowd away to find lodging and food.
13. Jesus replied, "You give them something to eat." They showed him the two fish and five loaves.
14. Over 5,000 people were there. He said to have them sit in groups of 50.

15. The disciples obeyed.
16. Jesus took the food, gave thanks, broke it, and gave it to the disciples to set before the people.
17. They all ate and were satisfied. They picked up 12 baskets of broken pieces left over so that none would be wasted.

Lessons:

10. If we report to Jesus, he will withdraw with us away from the crowds and the hustle and bustle of life to be with us.
11. Sometimes when we seek spiritual withdrawal, we have unexpected interruptions. These can be used as opportunities to witness about Jesus and to comfort others.
12. Sometimes we forget to rely on Jesus for the solution to our problems. We assume that we alone must come up with the resources to solve our problems.
13. Jesus wants us to feed his sheep with what little we have and when we are willing to do that he will multiply it.

14. Sometimes things seem impossible without Jesus. Jesus helps us to break down problems into smaller bite-sized pieces, and to organize and group things together.
15. We need to obey God and expect the best from him.
16. Jesus can take small things, small offerings, and turn them into something big. We need to be thankful and to use the small amount that we have. Also God expects us to participate in what he's doing.
17. When we offer everything we have to God and he multiplies it, we are more than satisfied with much left over. God can use broken pieces and broken people.

Questions:

10. Do I need to report to Jesus and let him withdraw me from the busyness of life more often?
11. Do I use interruptions in my day as opportunities to witness about Jesus and to comfort others?

Thank God in Advance

12. Do I rely on Jesus as the solution to my problems or have I been assuming that I must come up with my own resources to solve them?

13. Am I willing to give what little resources I have to God and trust him to multiply them to feed his sheep?

14. Do I fully realize that even things that seem impossible can be made possible through Jesus? Can I rely on Jesus to help me organize things and break down things that seem impossible?

15. Do I always obey God and expect the best from Him?

Live in Response:

> Dear Lord,
> Let me report to you, and let you withdraw me from the world. Let the interruption of my psychiatric disorder be an opportunity to witness to others. Teach me to rely on you, Jesus, as the solution to my problems, rather than assuming that I have to handle them all by myself.

I commit to trust you with what little resources I have so that you will multiply them to feed your sheep. I need to realize that the small amount I have can be a lot when put in God's hands. I just need to thank God for the blessings and the "nails" I have, as Ann Graham Lotz describes them, and to realize that the "nails" can be used as ways of witnessing to and comforting others.

I need to remember that I have a good mind, even though I have this disorder and that now that I have more frequent childcare each day, I can use my mind to discover what God wants me to do. God I love you so much. I have had many "nails" in my life, but I know that you have borne my pain, and I ask you to take my pain and let me be free of it each day in your glory.

God help me to know your will for me so that I can obey you and follow your direction in my life.

Help me Lord to be charitable to others and yet to keep my own integrity.

Love, Diana

9-18-09

John 14:1-4

1. Don't let your heart be troubled. Trust in God and Jesus.
2. In God's home there are many rooms, if this were not so I would have told you. I am going there to prepare a place for you.
3. And if I go, I will come back and take you with me so that you can be where I am.
4. You know the way to the place where I am going.

Lessons:

1. We need to trust in God and Jesus instead of letting our hearts be troubled. Don't worry about things in this world or the next for God has it planned out for you.
2. We need to trust that God has a place for us in heaven and that Jesus prepared this place for us when he died on the cross. Jesus is someone we can trust to tell us the truth about his Father's home.

3. When Jesus died on the cross, he also rose again and will take us to our eternal place in heaven to be with him.
4. We know the way to heaven because we know Jesus.

Questions:

1. If I knew the extent to how much happier I would be, how much more would I be willing to trust in Jesus?
2. How often do I let my heart be troubled instead of trusting in God and Jesus?
3. Do I completely trust Jesus that I will have an eternal home in heaven?
4. How well do I know Jesus?

Live in Response:

> Dear Lord,
> Thank you for this method of Bible Study taught by Anne Graham Lotz. Bless her a thousand fold. Help me to trust in Jesus more and more every day. Keep my heart from being troubled and

allow me to completely and fully trust your promise of my eternal home in your heavenly kingdom. Forgive me of my sins. Thank you God for keeping me strong in my faith. Help me use my time wisely now that my son is in school.

Love, Diana

9-19-09

Dear God,

Thank you for helping things to go better. Bless my husband and give him peace. I am happy knowing that I have a savior and best friend in Jesus Christ. I can count on you Jesus anytime or place, and you are always with me. I glorify your name. I repent of my sins and ask you to burn away all impurities in my soul. Make me a child after your own heart. Thank you for removing practically all of my troubling thoughts! This is an answer to prayer.

Thank you for giving me a good relationship with Mamaw. Bless her and help her to live a long happy life. Help keep her in good heath. Take special care of my mother-in-law too.

Take care of my oldest autistic son and give him a miracle God! Help him learn to talk normally. Let my daughter be drawn to you and to learn that you are the only way to eternal life. Put meaning and purpose in my life and help me to know how to successfully use my time to become closer to you. Help my mom find that Jesus is the only way to heaven. Help us grow closer together and grant us both peace.

Love, Diana

Psalm 19:14

"Let the words of my mouth and the meditation of my heart be acceptable in thy sight O Lord, my strength, and my redeemer."

Lord, Let me think better thoughts about myself, and take every thought captive to Christ. Help me to dwell on Philippians 4:8:

"Finally, brothers, whatever is true, whatever is noble, whatever is right, whatever is pure, whatever is lovely, whatever is admirable—if anything is excellent or praiseworthy—think about such things."

Lord, let me place you and all your excellent qualities on the throne of my soul instead of myself.

9-21-09

Dear Lord,

Today is my daughter's first day of college. Bless her Lord and surround her with your angels of protection. Guide her and give her wisdom and discernment. Help her to focus and concentrate on her studies and help her to be happy. Bless my oldest son in his comings and goings today and bless my youngest son as well.

Thank you Lord for the peace of mind you have given me. Help me to think on my feet more. Thank you for taking care me and loving me every day. Help me to be truthful always.

Love, Diana

9-23-09

Dear Lord,

Please keep my daughter safe and let no harm come to her. Help me to communicate with her better and help us to become more open with one another. Forgive me God for feeing angry about my disorder. I ask you to take away any thing about me that is not pleasing in your sight. Thank you for giving me such great peace of mind the past few weeks. I feel more calm. It is an answer to prayer.

Love, Diana

9-24-09

Dear Lord,

Please keep my daughter safe and protected from harm.

Love, Diana

9-25-09

Dear Lord,

Take care of my husband and help his textbook to go smoothly. Help me to have purpose and meaning in my life. Take away all the things in me that are impure in your sight. Take away all my negative unrealistic bad thoughts about myself. Replace them with positive, pure, and good thoughts about you and your handiwork. Forgive me of my sins, and bless me Lord. In Jesus's name, Amen.

Love, Diana

9-28-09

Dear Lord,

Thank you for helping me today. I pray that you will give me a new project to work on. I'm not sure if I want to work on a screenplay or simply on a story, possibly about myself. I can see myself working on the computer writing, but I would like it to be a project that others could benefit from. Lord, I pray for guidance about what I should do. Forgive me of my sins and take care of me. Keep my mind clear so that I can start and complete a project that glorifies Jesus Christ. Make me a pure blank paper on which you can write to fulfill your wishes for me.

Love, Diana

Dr. Diana Wilcox

9-29-09

First Day of Writing *Thank God in Advance*

Revelation 1:1-3

1. The revelation of Jesus Christ, which God gave him to show his servants what must soon take place. He made it known by sending his angel to his servant John.
2. Who testifies to everything he saw—that is, the word of God and the testimony of Jesus Christ.
3. Blessed is the one who reads the words of the prophecy, and blessed are those who hear it and take to heart what is written in it, because the time is near.

Lessons:

1. If we look to God's Word as his servants we can get a new revelation of Jesus Christ.
2. It is right to testify about God's word and Jesus.
3. Those who listen and obey God's word about prophecy will be blessed.

Thank God in Advance

Questions:

1. Am I always looking to God's word for a fresh vision of Jesus?
2. How can I testify more to others about God's word and Jesus?
3. If I knew all the ways I would be blessed by knowing about God's prophecies would I study them more?

Live in Response:

> Dear Lord,
> Let me look for a fresh revelation of Jesus in your Word and prophecies. Help me to develop better vehicles for testifying about Jesus.
>
> Love, Diana

9-30-09

Revelation 1:4:8

4. John, To the seven churches in the province of Asia: Grace and peace to you from him who

is, and who was, and who is to come, and from the seven spirits before his throne.

5. and from Jesus Christ, who is the faithful witness, the firstborn from the dead, and the ruler of the kings of the earth. To him who loves us and has freed us from our sins by his blood

6. and has made us to be a kingdom and priests to serve his God and Father—to him be glory and power for ever and ever! Amen.

7. Look, he is coming with the clouds, and every eye will see him, even those who pierced him, and all the peoples of the earth will mourn because of him. So shall it be! Amen.

8. "I am the Alpha and the Omega," says the Lord God, "who is, and who was, and who is to come, the Almighty."

Lessons:

4. God, the Holy Spirit and Jesus Christ all offer us peace.

5. You can count on what Jesus says. We must be obedient to him. He loved us so much that he died for our sins to be forgiven.

Thank God in Advance

6. Jesus has organized us into a body to serve him.
7. Even those who dislike Jesus will see him return.
8. The Lord is the beginning and the end, the past, present, and future.

Questions:

4. Do I ever seek peace from other things or people besides Jesus and God?
5. Do I count on what Jesus says? Do I completely realize Jesus's great love for me?
6. Do I appreciate the church community: How am I serving God? What if everyone in the church community served God as much as I did? Would that be a good thing?
7. Am I completely ready for Jesus's return? How can I warn others?
8. How can I comprehend the vastness of God?

Live In Response:

> Dear Lord,
> Help me to rely only on you (not things, food, finances, or other people)

for peace. Help me to meditate on your great vastness and majesty.

Love, Diana

10-1-09

Revelation 1: 9-12a

9. I, John, your brother and companion in the suffering and kingdom and patient endurance that are ours in Jesus, was on the island of Patmos because of the word of God and the testimony of Jesus.

10. On the Lord's Day I was in the Spirit, and I heard behind me a loud voice like a trumpet.

11. Which said: "Write on a scroll what you see and send it to the seven churches: to Ephesus, Smyrna, Pergamum, Thyatiram Sardis, Philadelphia and Laodicea."

12A. I turned around to see the voice that was speaking to me.

Lessons:

9. We sometimes have to suffer for serving Christ, but we can endure it with patience.

10. It's important to be in the Spirit even in suffering in order to hear the Lord's voice.
11. The Lord has important news for his church. We may be given news for his church.
12A. We need to turn toward Jesus to hear his voice.

Questions:

9. How should I handle it when I am suffering for having served Christ?
10. How patient am I about remaining in the Spirit when I am suffering so that I can hear God's voice?
11. How often do I obey God's word when he has important news for me to convey?
12A. Do I always turn to Jesus when I hear his voice?

Revelation 1:12b-16

12B. And when I turned I saw seven golden lampstands.
13. And among the lampstands was someone "like a son of man," dressed in a robe reach-

ing down to his feet and with a golden sash around his chest.

14. His head and hair were white like wool, and white as snow and his eyes were like blazing fire.

15. His feet were like bronze glowing in a furnace and his voice was like the sound of rushing waters.

16. In his right hand he held seven stars, and out of his mouth came a sharp double-edged sword. His face was like the sun shining in all its brilliance.

Lessons:

12B. When we turn toward Jesus, He reveals himself to us.

13. Jesus stands in the light, illuminating our understanding.

14. Jesus is pure and His eyes are able to see all, to blaze into us.

15. Jesus's feet are able to withstand the heat of a furnace of suffering, and His voice is powerful and strong like rushing waters.

Thank God in Advance

16. Jesus holds the heavens in His hands. His word cuts through darkness and his countenance shines like the sun.

Questions:

12B. How often do I truly turn toward Jesus when I am suffering unjustly? Is that always my first impulse?

13. When do I let Jesus illuminate my understanding of my issues?

14. How would my thoughts be different if I fully realized that Jesus could always see what I was thinking?

15. Do I recognize how much Jesus can identify with my suffering and how powerful he is to help and to enable me?

16. Do I recognize the great majesty of Jesus and the power of His Word and the brilliance of His countenance?

Live in Response:

> Lord, please give me new insight into my issues. Please purify my thoughts and

actions with your word and the presence
of your majesty and brilliance.

Revelation 1:17-19

17. When I saw him, I fell at his feet as though dead. Then he placed his right hand on me and said: "Do not be afraid. I am the First and the Last."

18. I am the Living One; I was dead, and behold I am alive forever and ever! And I hold the keys of death and Hades.

19. "Write, therefore, what you have seen, what is now and what will take place later."

Lessons:

17. When we see Jesus we fall at His feet in worship and His Word comforts us for He is the first and the last.

18. Even though Jesus was once dead, He is now alive forever and holds the keys to our eternal destiny.

19. It is good to write down your observations of God's glory, especially when He tells you to do so.

Thank God in Advance

Questions:

17. How is my life changing because of the fresh vision that I have had of Jesus Christ? In what ways are the changes in my life equivalent to falling at His feet and yet responding to His comforting peace?
18. Do I completely realize how powerful Jesus is in holding the key to my death and to my eternal destiny?
19. Should I be writing down my experiences of visions with Jesus more so that I can better realize His glory in my life and share that glory with others?

Live in Response:

> Dear Lord,
> Let me take the power of Jesus over my destiny more seriously. Let me write about my vision of His glory to realize that glory in my life and to magnify His holy name to others. I commit to study God's Word more everyday. I will stay in the Spirit so that I may hear God's voice. I will continue with my journal called

Dr. Diana Wilcox

> Thank God in Advance, which documents my life and my becoming and developing as a Christian. I will ask Jesus to give me new insight into my life and to enable me to glorify His name to others. Lord, please continue to direct me and provide a deeper relationship with you. Please help me to keep my commitment of doing Bible study every day.
>
> Love, Diana

Revelation 2:1-7

1. To the angel of the church in Ephesus write: These are the words of him who holds the seven stars in his right hand and walks among the seven golden lampstands:

2. I know your deeds, your hard work and your perseverance. I know that you cannot tolerate wicked men, that you have tested those who claim to be apostles but are not and have found them false.

3. You have persevered and have endured hardships for my name, and have not grown weary.

4. Yet I hold this against you: You have forsaken your first love.

5. Remember the height from which you have fallen! Repent and do the things you did at first. If you do not repent, I will come to you and remove your lampstand from its place.

6. But you have this in your favor: You hate the practices of the Nicolaitans, which I also hate.

7. He who has an ear; let him hear what the Spirit says to the churches. To him who overcomes, I will give the right to eat from the tree of life, which is in the paradise of God.

Lessons:

1. Jesus illuminates our understanding of His presence through His written word.

2. Jesus knows all our deeds, perseverance, and hard work.

3. Jesus recognizes the hardships that we endure for His name.

4. Jesus holds it against us when we have forsaken our first love, Jesus Christ.

5. Jesus reminds us of the height from which we've fallen in forsaking Him and neglecting Him. We must repent and return to a loving

childlike understanding and acceptance of Jesus.

6. Jesus hates evil practices.
7. Listen to the Lord. If you repent and overcome you will live eternally.

Questions:

1. If Jesus illuminates our understanding of His presence through His written Word, would I feel His presence more in my life if I read my Bible more?
2. Do I fully thank Jesus for acknowledging all my deeds, perseverance, and hard work?
3. Do I fully appreciate Jesus for recognizing all the hardships that I've endured in His name?
4. Have I forsaken my first love, Jesus Christ, by neglecting my Bible reading, and not spending enough time with Him in prayer?
5. How can I return to the height of love for Jesus from which I have fallen? How can I go back and do the things I used to do when I was most in love with Him?

6. Do I have the same hatred for evil practices that Jesus does?

7. How can I fully repent and overcome and fall completely in love with Jesus all over again?

Live in Response:

> Lord,
>
> The scripture is true. I have forsaken my first love. I hereby commit to spend more time alone with Jesus in His word, in prayer, and serving Him, and glorifying His name to others.
>
> Love, Diana

10-2-09

Jeremiah 29:11

I know the plans I have for you declares the Lord, "Plans to prosper you and not to harm you, plans to give you hope and a future."

Lessons:

We can trust God to prosper us, not to harm us, and to give us hope and a future.

Dr. Diana Wilcox

Questions:

How can I have a vision of God's plan for my life? Do I completely trust God to prosper me and to keep me safe, to give me hope and a future?

Live in Response:

> Dear Lord,
> I pray to you to help me trust you in all these areas and to embrace and thank you in advance for your glorious plan for my life!
>
> Thank you God! So far I have written seventeen pages in four days on the *Thank God in Advance* project. Please guide me about what to write as I feel that I am developing a closer relationship with Jesus. The Bible study developed by Anne Graham Lotz has truly helped.
>
> Love, Diana

Revelation 3:1-6

1. To the angel of the church in Sardis write: These are the words of him who holds the seven spirits of God and the seven stars. I

know your deeds; you have a reputation of being alive, but you are dead.

2. Wake up! Strengthen what remains and is about to die, for I have not found your deeds complete in the sight of God.

3. Remember, therefore, what you have received and heard; obey it and repent. But if you do not wake up, I will come like a thief, and you will not know at what time I will come to you.

4. Yet you have a few people in Sardis who have not soiled their clothes. They will walk with me, dressed in white, for they are worthy.

5. He who overcomes will, like them, be dressed in white. I will never blot out his name from the book of life but will acknowledge his name before my Father and his angels.

6. He who has an ear; let him hear what the Spirit says to the churches.

Lessons:

1. Even though we appear to be alive, many of us are dead inside. We are just going through the motions, safe in our comfort zone.

2. We need to wake up and strengthen our spirit that remains, for our deeds are not complete in God's eyes.

3. We need to obey and repent or else God may come for our lives if we refuse to live fully for Him.

4. There were only a few people in the church of Sardis who were worthy to walk with the Lord. This may be true for modern day churches too.

5. If we overcome and repent, Jesus will not blot out our name from the book of Life and will acknowledge us before His Father in heaven.

6. Jesus warns us to listen to His Word.

Questions:

1. Even though I am alive, am I really dead inside? Am I too comfortable in my comfort zone, just going through the motions of life?

2. If I realized how many of my deeds were not complete in God's eyes, to what extent would I wake up and strengthen what remains of my spirit?

3. Lord, if I don't live my life fully for you, do you plan to come like a thief for me?
4. Am I worthy to walk with Jesus? How can I make myself more worthy?
5. How much strength would I gain if I fully realized how important it was to repent and overcome, so that Jesus will acknowledge me to God in heaven?
6. How often do I truly listen to and obey Jesus's Word?

Live in Response:

> Dear Lord,
>
> Let me stop feeling dead inside. I don't want to be like the fig tree with leaves but no fruit. When Jesus found it had nothing but leaves, He said, "May you never bear fruit again!" Immediately the tree withered (See Matthew 21:18-19). Lord take me out of the wilderness of my comfort zone and lead me to the Promised Land that you have in store for me. I need to wake up! My deeds are not complete in God's eyes!
>
> Love, Diana

Revelation 3:7-13

7. To the angel of the church in Philadelphia write: These are the words of him who is holy and true, who holds the key of David. What he opens no one can shut, and what he shuts no one can open.

8. I know your deeds. See I have placed before you an open door that no one can shut. I know that you have little strength, yet you have kept my word and have not denied my name.

9. I will make those who are of the synagogue of Satan, who claim to be Jews though they are not but are liars—I will make them come and fall down at your feet and acknowledge that I have loved you.

10. Since you have kept my command to endure patiently, I will also keep you from the hour of trial that is going to come upon the whole world to test those who live on the earth.

11. I am coming soon. Hold on to what you have, so that no one will take your crown.

12. Him who overcomes I will make a pillar in the temple of my God. Never again will he leave it. I will write on him the name of my

Thank God in Advance

God and the name of the city of my God, the new Jerusalem, which is coming down out of heaven from my God, and I will also write on him my new name.

13. He who has an ear; let him hear what the Spirit says to the churches.

Lessons:

7. Jesus alone has the power to open or shut doors of opportunity for each of us.
8. Jesus knows our deeds. A door of opportunity is open to some of us that no one can shut. Even though some of us have little strength, we have kept God's word and not denied His name.
9. Those who claim to be righteous, but are liars, will fall at the feet of the righteous and acknowledge Jesus's love for them.
10. If we obey and endure patiently, we won't go through the hour of trial to test the world.
11. Jesus is coming soon. Hold on to your faith, so that no one may take it from you.

12. You will be a pillar in God's temple and never leave it. Jesus will write God's name on you.
13. Listen to what God has to say!

Questions:

7. Do I ever rely on other things or people besides Jesus to open doors of opportunity for me? How can I learn to trust Jesus alone to open doors of opportunity for me?
8. What people in my life claim to be righteous but are liars? Will those people repent?
9. How can I obey Jesus completely and endure the pressures of life more patiently?
10. How can I have more spiritual strength to hold on to what I have so that no one takes my crown of faith?
11. How can I become a pillar in God's temple so that when people see me they will see God's name written on me?
12. Do I completely listen and take in all that Jesus has to say?

Live in Response:

> Dear Lord,
>
> Teach me not to rely on other things or people to open doors of opportunity for me. Let me rely solely on you. Let me realize that my writing Thank God in Advance is a door of opportunity. Help me to obey Jesus completely and to endure the pressures of life more patiently. Let me gain spiritual strength from reading and studying my Bible. Allow some people in my life to repent. Allow me to hold on to my crown of faith. Teach me to listen to you completely and to take in and remember all that Jesus has to say.
>
> Love, Diana

10-3-09

Revelation 3:14-22

> 14. To the angel of the church in Laodicea write: These are the words of the Amen, the faithful and true witness, the ruler of God's creation.

15. I know your deeds, that you are neither cold nor hot. I wish you were either one or the other!
16. So because you are lukewarm—neither hot or cold—I am about to spit you out of my mouth.
17. You say, "I am rich; I have acquired wealth and do not need a thing." But you do not realize that you are wretched, pitiful, poor, blind, and naked.
18. I counsel you to buy from me gold refined in the fire so you can become rich; and white clothes to wear so you can cover your shameful nakedness; and salve to put on your eyes, so you can see.
19. Those who I love I rebuke and discipline. So be earnest, and repent.
20. Here I am! I stand at the door and knock. If anyone hears my voice and opens the door, I will come in and eat with him and he with me.
21. To him who overcomes, I will give the right to sit with me on my throne, just as I overcame and sat down with my Father on his throne.

22. He who has an ear, let him hear what the Spirit says to the churches.

Lessons:

14. Listen to Jesus for He is the faithful and true witness, the ruler of God's creation.
15. Jesus knows when we are neutral and apathetic about Him, and He can't stand it!
16. In fact, when we are lukewarm about Jesus, He wants to "spit us out!"
17. Sometimes we are deceived by our material wealth when we are really quite poor in spirit.
18. We need to spend time with Jesus and gain in golden wisdom refined by suffering for His name, purity of spirit to cover our sins, and vision for our lives.
19. If God disciplines us, we can be sure that it is because He loves us.
20. Jesus is always present with us. He stands at the door of our soul and knocks. If we hear His voice and open the door, He'll come in and commune with us.

21. If we overcome, we will sit with Jesus on His throne.
22. If we are wise, we will listen to what Jesus says.

Questions:

14. Do I fully realize that Jesus is the only faithful and true witness?
15. To what extent am I just neutral about God's Word?
16. How can I be more passionate about Jesus and His Word?
17. Do I rely on other things besides Jesus to give me richness and passion in life?
18. Could more Bible study and prayer help me to come richer with God's refined wisdom, purer in spirit and greater in vision?
19. Is God using this opportunity to discipline me?
20. Do I need to let Jesus into my heart more than I already do?
21. Do I still need to repent for neglecting my Bible reading?
22. Do I listen enough to Jesus?

Live in Response:

Dear Lord,

Let me be more passionate about Jesus and look to the Bible and prayer for greater wisdom, purity and vision. I accept God's discipline of me and repent that I need to read the Bible more and spend more time in prayer. I want to overcome. I pray that I will wake up and stop going through the motions in my life and be more passionate about Jesus and His Word. I will pray and study my Bible more. I will hold on to my crown and not waiver from my faith. I will continue writing *Thank God in Advance* as a door of opportunity and see my life itself as a door of opportunity. I will continue to pray and study my Bible every day. Lord, please help me keep my commitment to you and give me continued direction and a deeper relationship with you.

Love, Diana

10-4-09

Dear Lord,

I have come to a stopping point in my project. Please help me to keep writing. I've written twenty pages so far. Thank you for convicting me of my sins and helping me to repent. I don't want to just go through the motions in my life. I need your help, Lord, to step out of the boat and strengthen myself spiritually and to purify my mind. Lord, I ask you to refine me in your own way that I may come to have your golden wisdom. Purify me so that my heart is as white as snow. Give me salve for my eyes so that I might have vision in my life. Lord, I long for your vision and purpose. I long to serve you.

I also pray for a few good friends. Teach me how to make friends more easily Lord. Take care of my friends who are ill and give them a quick recovery.

Lord, take any rebellious spirit in me and turn it around to use for your glory. Forgive me of my sins and purify my heart, mind, speech, and actions. Teach me to be more comfortable praying aloud in front of others. Give me courage

Thank God in Advance

and give me precision of right thinking and right speech. Help me to glorify only you and you alone.

Give me the peace that passes all understanding. For you did not give me a "spirit of timidity, but a spirit of power, of love, and of self-discipline" (2 Timothy 1:7).

Thank you for taking care of my husband. Give him peace and help his work to go smoothly. Let neither one of us be tempted to go astray from the other. Keep our marriage strong and full of faith. Give him strength, courage, and faith. Help him everyday. Glory, power, and honor to you Almighty God. Thank you for giving us your great Son and for forgiving us of our sins. May you find comfort in our meager offerings of love.

Love, Diana

10-5-09

Romans 12:14-16

14. Bless those who persecute you, bless and do not curse.

15. Rejoice with those who rejoice, mourn with those who mourn.
16. Live in harmony with one another. Do not be proud. But be willing to associate with people of low position. Do not be conceited.

Lessons:

14. We should bless and not curse those who persecute us.
15. Even if they are the ones persecuting us, we should rejoice when others rejoice and mourn when others mourn.
16. We need to live in harmony without being proud or conceited, always being willing to associate with those of low position.

Questions:

14. How can I bless those who have persecuted me in my life more?
15. Can I be more empathic with them in times of sadness and rejoicing?
16. How can I live in better harmony with people? Can I learn to humble myself as a servant?

Live in Response:

> Dear Lord,
>
> Let me bless those who have persecuted me or cast me aside more. Help me to humble myself as a servant. Lord, please direct me, and let me know what, if anything you would have me write about. Do you want me to write about my life? Will I upset others if I write about them? God answered, "Sincere love makes other people better persons." Perhaps that is what this is also about, for me to become a better person. I will consider the possibility that this book *Thank God in Advance* is also for others. So far I have written twenty pages on the computer. Lord, guide me and give me wisdom about what the book should be about—Lord, please use me as a vessel, as a servant to glorify you.
>
> Love, Diana

John 15:5-8

5. I am the true vine. I am the vine; you are the branches. If a man remains in me and I in him, he will bear much fruit, apart from me you can do nothing.

6. If you don't remain in me, you'll be like a branch that is thrown away and withers and is burned.

7. If you remain in me and my words remain in you, ask whatever you wish and it will be given to you.

8. This is to God's glory, that you bear much fruit, showing yourselves to be my disciples.

Lessons:

5. We must remain in Jesus in order to bear fruit.

6. We will die and spend eternity in hell if we are apart from Jesus.

7. If we remain in Jesus, whatever we wish will be given to us.

8. This is not for our glory, but for God's glory, that we bear much fruit and show ourselves to be Christ's disciples.

Questions:

5. If I knew the kind of fruit I could bear, to what extent would I remain more in Jesus? And how can I remain in Him more?

6. Who do I know who is apart from Jesus and how can I help them?
7. If I remain in Jesus, what kind of fruit will I wish for? To write a book?
8. How can I always put God's glory first? How can I realize that God wants me to bear much fruit to show myself as his disciple?

Live in Response:

> Dear Lord,
> I want to remain in Jesus and to bear fruit. Lord, help me to remain closer to you through your Word and through prayer. Forgive me for neglecting my Bible reading and my prayer in the past. Help me to commit to do better. I pray for my family and friends who are apart from Jesus. Lord, I pray that I may increase in all of the fruits of the Spirit, and that I may write, complete, publish, and successfully market a book that glorifies you and your name. Help me to always glorify you, so that I may show myself as your disciple.

Lord, help me get out of the rut that I've been in and please let me know what fruits you would like for me to bear.

Jesus, forgive me for the times in the past when I've rejected you and forsaken you, and disobeyed you. I deserved the discipline you gave me and more. I was wrong and I humbly ask you to forgive me in your name. It is terrible to be apart from you. Please guide me so that I may remain steadfastly in you always. I feel contrite for my sins. Thank you for forgiving me.

Love, Diana

10-6-09

John 3:3,5-6

3. I tell you the truth; no one can see the kingdom of God unless he is born again

5. ...no one can enter the kingdom of God unless he is born of water and the Spirit.

6. Flesh gives birth to flesh, but the Spirit gives birth to spirit.

Thank God in Advance

Lessons:

3. We must be born again in the Spirit in order to see God's kingdom in heaven.
5. We can't enter God's kingdom unless we are born of Jesus's living water and the Holy Spirit.
6. Only Jesus can give birth to our spirit, and we must be born through Him to enter God's kingdom.

Questions:

3. How can I help others to be born again?
5. …How can I share Jesus's living water and Holy Spirit with others?
6. How can I write about how only Jesus can give birth to the spirit?

Live in Response:

> Dear Lord,
> I will use this passage in my writing. I want to share Jesus's living water and Holy Spirit with others.
>
> Love, Diana

God said to me:
Diana,
You have repented of your sins, and I am proud of you. Read and listen to my word. I have plans for you.

> Dear Lord,
>
> Thank you for all the joy and peace you've given me. Help me to use my past burdens to be a light to others. Forgive me of my sins. Help me to remember all your "benefits" (Psalm 103:2) in my afflictions and as I sort through the archives of my memories of my life. Give me a "crown of beauty instead of ashes, the oil of gladness instead of mourning, and a garment of praise instead of a spirit of despair (Isaiah 61:3)." "Redeem my life from the pit and crown me with love and compassion (Psalm 103:4)." As I write *Thank God in Advance*, help me to speak truth into my soul and see God's benefits even in the most painful memories.
>
> Love, Diana

10-7-09

2 Corinthians 1:3-4

3. Praise to God and Father of Jesus Christ, the Father of all compassion and the God of all comfort
4. Who comforts us in all our troubles, so that we can comfort those in any trouble with the comfort we ourselves have received from God.

Lessons:

3. We need to look only to God and Jesus as the source of all compassion and comfort.
4. God comforts us in our troubles so that we can, in turn, comfort others in *any* trouble with the *same* comfort we have received from God.

Questions:

3. Do I sometimes look to other sources of comfort and compassion, such as food or friends?
4. How can I receive God's comfort more in my own life, so that I can turn that around and comfort others? How can I comfort others in my writing?

Live in Response:

Dear Lord,

Help me to seek compassion and comfort only from you. I praise you for the compassion and comfort you have given me in my troubles. Lord, let me review my life through the light of your comfort and compassion so that I may draw new compassion from my situation to share with others in their times of trouble, all to glorify you, for you are my sanctuary. Lord Jesus, I praise your majesty above all things; I praise you as the Creator of the universe, as the omnipotent and omniscient God! Thank you for your all-knowing comfort.

In John 16:23-24, you command me to ask something in your name. "And in that day you will ask me nothing. Most assuredly, I say to you, whatever you ask the Father in My name he will give you. Until now you have asked nothing in my name. Ask and you will receive, that your joy may be full." Lord, I ask that you will give me clarity and confidence to write a book about my life without you and with you, my testimony, and Christian walk. Please give me the ability to organize my thoughts into chapters. Give me peace. Also please help me get over my tendency to use food as a comfort instead of coming to you Jesus.

For my writing, please help my memory, and help me remember some good things, good times to write about too. Just guide me Lord, in my steps, for you know far better than I do what I should do. I pray that you will increase my vision for my life, and give me new confidence to write and also to speak before others and especially to organize my thoughts into a coherent book. Take care of all my children and lead them and my mother closer to Christ, my brother also. And bless my grandmother, mother-in-law, and sister-in-law.

Love, Diana

God said to me:

Diana,
I want to tell you today that I love you and that I am sorry for all that you

have been through. Joy and comfort and treasures in heaven will be yours as you continue to live your life for me. Listen to your heart, and you will know what to write. Organize your thoughts into chapters by your songs, and it will be easier. Blessings on you and your family.

Love, God

10-8-09

Dear Lord,

I choose to make you, rather than me, the center of my life and my thoughts. Help me to praise and glorify you throughout the day. I pray for my mother to come closer to Jesus and Jesus alone. Thank you, God, for giving me health. Bless all my family and draw them closer to you.

Love, Diana

Dear Jesus,

I ask you to give me a better knowledge and memory of the Bible and your Word. Help me to draw closer to you and to seek only you. I ask you to give me the creative flow that will magnify you and you only.

Love, Diana

10-9-09

Mark 12:30-31

- 30. Love the Lord your God with all your heart and with all your soul and with all your mind and with all your strength.
- 31. The second is this: Love your neighbor as yourself. There is no commandment greater than these.

Lessons:

- 30. We must love the Lord with all that we have and not be double-minded about it. We must love him whole-heartedly.
- 31. We are God's handiwork, and we must love our neighbors and ourselves as God's handiwork.

Questions:

30. How can I love the Lord with more of my heart, more of my soul, more of my mind, and more of my strength?
31. How can I learn to love myself and my neighbor more as God's precious and honored handiwork?

Live in Response:

> Dear Lord,
>
> Let me love you more. Give me a bigger heart to love you more. Broaden my soul's depths to love you deeper. Sharpen and clarify my mind to love you more clearly. Strengthen my spirit that I may love you more strongly. Forgive my sins and enlarge the territory of my deep love for you. Let me learn to love myself as your temple and handiwork more, so that I may in turn love others more as your temples and precious handiwork. Give me joy overflowing from your wellspring of life.
>
> Help me to fulfill these two greatest and all of your Ten Commandments. Let

Thank God in Advance

me not be tempted to be led astray. Help me in my weakness, for in my weakness you are strong. Lord, I praise you. I love you with all my heart, mind, strength, and soul. I worship you and you alone. You are the King of Kings and the Lord of Lords. Thank you for hearing my cries and for rescuing me from danger and from a life of sin and loneliness. I have missed you. Bless Trinity Broadcasting Network for leading me back to you. Bless my husband for being such a good Christian example. Bless my family and friends.

Lord, I ask you to make me your servant, humble and willing to discipline myself to serve you. I ask that you allow me to minister to others by writing a book about my Christian walk. Please use your blazing vision to give me insight on what to write about and how to organize it.

Please let it be a way to encourage others to walk with you in times of trouble. I commit to continue to get up early in the mornings and study my Bible and to pray to your Lord, so that I may have a deeper relationship with you.

Love, Diana

10-10-09

Luke 6:37-38

37. Do not judge, and you will not be judged. Do not condemn, and you will not be condemned. Forgive and you will be forgiven.

38. Give and it will be given to you. A good measure, pressed down, shaken together, and running over will be poured into your lap. For with the measure you use, it will be measured to you.

Lessons:

37. We must not judge others, or we will be judged. We must not condemn others, or we will be condemned. Instead we must forgive others, and then we can be forgiven.

38. If you give, it will be given to you. God will give back a measure overflowing into your lap, exactly by the measure you use. Be generous with God's children, and He will be generous to you.

Questions:

37. How can I get closer to God so that I will not ever judge or condemn others? Have I truly forgiven those in my life who have hurt me?

38. How can I be more generous with God's children?

Live in Response:

> Dear Lord,
>
> Allow me to draw closer to you so that I will not judge or condemn other people. Forgive me for the times I have done this. Help me to truly forgive those in my life who have hurt me. Help me know what aspects of my life to include in the book *Thank God in Advance*. It's not my intention to hurt anyone in my writing; it's only to show how I have overcome my suffering through a deeper relationship with Jesus Christ.
>
> Also help me to be generous with God's children, so that I may receive your love more abundantly. Teach me not to judge and condemn myself too! Now that is a big one! It is challenging

not to condemn myself in the same way that some people seem to condemn me. Forgive them and forgive me, for I must press on!

Please help me to do your will in my writing. Help me to write a Christian inspiration book called something like *Thank God in Advance*, if it be your will. I praise you for helping me to write the first thirty pages. Please help me to organize my thoughts and to let the creativity flow even more. Forgive me of all my sins and help me to recover from a life of past sin. Lead me closer and closer to you in a life of joy, comfort, and peace. I ask you father God, to be generous with your humble servant and to let me complete, publish, and successfully market this book. Forgive my sins and rebellious thoughts for you are my Lord of lords, the God of all creation, King of kings. Please guide me each step of the way.

                              Love, Diana

10-11-09

Mark 10:43-45

43. Instead whoever wants to become great among you must be your servant
44. And whoever wants to be first must be a slave to all.
45. For even the Son of Man did not come to be served, but to serve, and to give his life as a ransom for many.

Lessons:

43. If you want to be great among people, you must first be their servant.
44. If you want to be first, you must be a slave to all.
45. Jesus, who is supreme above all men, himself did not come to be served, but to serve, to the point of dying on a cross for the sins of all humanity.

Questions:

43. In my writing *Thank God in Advance* and in my daily life, how can I be more of a servant to others?

44. How can I be a slave to others in my writing and in my life?

45. Do I fully appreciate Jesus's example as a servant to others? Do I always follow his example?

Live in Response:

> Dear Lord,
>
> Teach me to follow Jesus's shining example of being a servant to others in my daily life and in my writing of *Thank God in Advance*. Take away my selfishness and my pride. Help me to build a lighthouse of God's Word for others who need God's help if it be your will.
>
> Bless my daughter and lead her to Jesus. Bless my sons and all our descendants and lead them to you. Bless my friends and family. Jesus, like blind Bartimeus (Mark 10:46-52), I want to see what you have for me in my life to do that I may bring glory to your name. Please wash away any impurities in my heart, mind, and soul that are displeasing to you. Forgive me of my sins and help me to become a better steward of my time in relationship with you. I love you

so much Jesus. Bless my former husband and his family and lead them to you and your abundant favor. Bless my family. Keep us all safe and help us to thrive in your glory.

Love, Diana

10-12-09

Psalm 108:1-3

1. My heart is steadfast, O God;
2. Awake, harp and lyre!
3. I will awaken the dawn.
4. I will praise you, O Lord, among the nations, I will sing of you among the peoples.

Lessons:

1. Keep your heart steadfast on God.
2. Sing and make music with all your soul! Make music with harp and lyre! Awake!
3. Awaken the dawn with praise for the Lord!
4. Praise the Lord among the nations. Sing of the Lord among the peoples.

Questions:

1. How can I keep my heart more steadfast on God? Should I be singing and making music with my soul more?

2. How can I tap into the joy of praising the Lord with song more? Have I been discouraged about singing since I am only just beginning to market my CD? How can I "awaken the dawn" with praise for my Lord by singing? Is my heart in it?

3. Do I need to get past the discouragement of just beginning to market my CD and just praise the Lord through my singing "among the peoples" anyway?

Live in Response:

> Dear Lord,
> Help me keep my heart steadfast on you by singing and making music. Help me to give the discouragement I have felt over the meager beginnings of my CD sales over to you. I put it in you hands. Help me to enjoy singing my songs again. Help me to enjoy praising your

Thank God in Advance

> name through song. Father God, I have written thirty-two pages of my project, *Thank God in Advance*. Help me to come up with ideas for chapters and to organize the book into chapters. I would like for it to be a book to help others get over their emotional trauma as I have gotten over mine through Jesus Christ.

God said:
  Chapter ideas:

- Forgive yourself and forgive others
- Fall in love with Jesus
- The greatest two commandments
- The fruits of the spirit
- God uses broken pieces—come broken
- Be a servant to others, be humble
- Be faithful to God
- Walk the walk; dedicate all aspects of your life to God
- Sing a song of Joy
- Receive God's vision for your life

- Put on the armor of God
- Remain in Jesus (I am the Vine)
- Praise God

> Dear Lord,
> Please give me the mental clarity to write this book. Help me to get over my discouragement about just beginning to market my CD for there is no shame in meager beginnings.
>
> Love, Diana

10-13-09

2 Corinthians 1:3-4

3. Praise be to the God and Father of our Lord Jesus Christ, the father of all compassion and the God of all comfort,

4. Who comforts us in all our troubles, so that we can comfort those in any trouble with the comfort we ourselves have received from God.

Lessons:

3. We need to praise God for the compassion and comfort he gives us in times of trouble.

4. God comforts us in all our troubles so that we can comfort others in any trouble with the comfort we have received from God.

Questions:

3. How often do I praise God for the compassion and comfort He gives me?
4. If I took the time to comfort others more through my writing about God's comforting me, could I thank God in advance for a double portion of comfort and compassion?

Live in Response:

> Dear Lord,
> Let me praise you more for all the comfort and compassion you have shown me all my life. This will be my one of my first chapters—"Praising God for his Comfort and Compassion." Lord, I ask you to give me comfort and compassion as I write this book on my Christian walk to help others. Thank you, Lord, for the comfort you have given me, that I may in turn comfort others. I praise you Lord for answering my prayers of giv-

ing me more clarity of mind and more spiritual strength, and more ability to see your vision for my life. Thank you for the rain. Thank you for the sunshine. Thank you for my little boy and all his blessings. Help him to be happy at school.

Love, Diana

Jeremiah 31:13

13. Then maidens will dance and be glad, Young men and old as well. I will turn their mourning into gladness; I will give them comfort and joy instead of sorrow.

Lessons:

13. We should dance with joy for the Lord. Our Lord turns mourning into gladness and sorrow into comfort and joy.

Questions:

13. How often do I praise God and remember Him for how He turned my mourning into gladness and my sorrow into comfort and joy? How often do I tell others?

Live in Response:

> Dear Lord,
> Let me forever praise you for turning my sorrow and mourning into comfort and gladness! Take care of my brother and bless him with your abundant favor.
>
> Love, Diana

10-14-09

A Study on Brokenness:

> The sacrifices of God are a broken spirit; a broken and contrite heart O God, you will not despise.
>
> Psalm 51:17

> The Lord is close to the brokenhearted.
>
> Psalm 34:18

> He has sent me to bind up
> the brokenhearted.
>
> Isaiah 61:1

Dr. Diana Wilcox

> Dear Lord,
> Help me to write a chapter on coming to the Lord broken.
>
> Love, Diana

Isaiah 61:1, 7

1. The spirit of the sovereign Lord is on me, because the Lord has anointed me to preach good news to the poor. He has sent me to bind up the brokenhearted, to proclaim freedom for the captives and release from darkness for the prisoners, to proclaim the year of the Lord's favor, and the day of vengeance of our God, to comfort all who mourn, and provide for those who grieve in Zion—to bestow on them a crown of beauty instead of ashes, the oil of gladness instead of mourning, and a garment of praise instead of a spirit of despair. They will be called oaks of righteousness, a planting of the Lord for the display of his splendor.

7. …Instead of their shame my people will receive a double portion.

Lessons:

1. The Lord has anointed me to preach good news to the poor. I need to use my writing to

Thank God in Advance

bind up the brokenhearted, proclaim freedom to the captives, release prisoners from darkness, proclaim the year of the Lord's favor, and the day of his vengeance, comfort those who mourn and grieve, replace ashes, mourning, and despair with beauty, gladness, and praise. They will be righteous and will display the Lord's splendor.

7. Those who overcome in the Lord will receive a double portion for their shame.

Questions:

1. How can I become a better preacher of the good news? Do I need to be more passionate about preaching God's Word to others in my life and in my writing?

7. In what ways will I receive a double portion for my past shame?

Live in Response:

> Dear Lord,
> Let me read your Word more, and be inspired by your Word, so that I may be more passionate about preaching the gospel. I want to preach the year of your

favor and to comfort those who mourn and grieve. Thank you for the clarity of mind you have given me. It is an answer to prayer! Father, I praise you and thank you for your Word that has so inspired me. Thank you for all your great love and kindness. Bring a right spirit to me. Help me to write the book if it be your will. Lord, I commit to read your Word more so that I will be able to preach to others. Thank you for your inspiration and bless Anne Graham Lotz and her family for her inspiration. Give her her heart's desires.

I called the 700 Club for prayer about the book yesterday. Thank you for the counselor, Bonnie, and bless her and the 700 Club, as well as Pat Robertson and his family. Bless our church and pastors and staff and all their families. Bless our President and world leaders and lead them to peace for the world if it be your will.

Jesus, help me get over my fear of speaking and singing in public. Forgive me of my sins.

Love, Diana

10-15-09

Dear Lord,

Thank you for forgiving me of my sins. Bless my friends. Bless their comings and goings. Give them God's favor. Bless our missionary families too.

Love, Diana

10-16-09

Philippians 3:13-14

Forgetting what is behind and straining toward what is ahead, I press on toward the goal to win the prize for which God has called me heavenward in Christ Jesus.

Lessons:

We need to forget the past, and instead strain forward toward the future. This is the only way we will win the prize that God has for us. If we keep dwelling on the past and trying to undo it, we will be stuck in the past. Instead realize that after you repent, God has forgiven you. Have faith that he has forgiven you and then press on toward the future. If you keep dwelling on the past, you will not be able to see the vision that God has planned for you in your life.

Questions:

If I knew how much dwelling on the past has kept me from seeing God's vision for my life, would I have stopped sooner?

Live in Response:

> I accept God's forgiveness for my past sins, even though it is hard sometimes to forgive myself, I do forgive myself too. I will stop dwelling on the past and press on toward the future in Jesus's name.

> Love, Diana

1 Corinthians 1: 5-7

5. For in him you have been enriched in every way—in all your speaking and in all your knowledge
6. Because our testimony about Christ was confirmed in you.
7. Therefore you do not lack any spiritual gift.

Lessons:

5. This is addressed to all those who call on the name of the Lord Jesus Christ.
   It is exciting. It is a promise from God that in every way we have been enriched through Jesus Christ—in all our speaking and all our knowledge.
6. This is because of our testimony about him.
7. Because Jesus has enriched us in every way, we do not lack any spiritual gift.

Questions:

5. Has my speaking and my knowledge of God's Word been enriched as I have requested of God? Have these prayers been answered?
6. Has my giving my testimony helped to enrich my speaking and knowledge of God's Word?
7. What other spiritual gifts has Jesus given me? Do I claim this promise of being enriched in my speaking, knowledge, and spiritual gifts for myself?

Live in Response:

Dear Lord,

Help me practice my spiritual gifts of speaking, knowledge, writing, and whatever other gifts you have for me to use to your glory. Help me to overcome my shyness and my negative thoughts. Help me to think only positive thoughts in you.

Love, Diana

10-17-09

Dear Lord,

Make me a vessel for you and your Word. Thank you for helping me develop more friendships. That is an answer to prayer. Help me to start singing again if it be your will. Help me to write, complete, publish, and market this Christian inspiration book that I am writing. Help me to know more about what to write. Lord, let me know if you want me to advertise my music on the radio.

Love, Diana

Thank God in Advance

God said,
    No, write the book first.

> Lord,
>   Help me to be patient, and to know that recognition of my music for your glory will happen in your time.
>
>   Love, Diana

John 4:35 (My favorite Bible verse):

Do not say, "four months more and then the harvest?" I tell you, open your eyes and look at the fields! They are ripe for harvest.

Lessons:

Don't always say that your harvest of souls for God's kingdom is down the road. Look, your harvest is ready now!

Questions:

Am I ready to reap a harvest of souls for God's kingdom right now?

Am I prepared for what God has planned for me?

Live in Response:

Dear Lord,

Help me to be ready for the harvest you have for me. Prepare me for what you have planned for me. Guide me to sing as you plan. Guide me to write as you plan. It is all for your glory.

Love, Diana

10-17-09 (cont)

Dear Lord,

It has been about three weeks since I started writing *Thank God in Advance*, and I feel that I am at a stand still. I have written forty pages. Please give me the insight to continue writing. I claim Pastor Paula White's promise from you on her CD of increase and abundance! New doors of opportunity will open in the name of Jesus!

10-18-09

2 Timothy 6-7

For this reason I remind you to fan into flame the gift of God which is in you, through the laying on of hands. For God did not give us a spirit of timidity, but a spirit of power, of love, and of self-discipline.

Lessons:

We should ask for prayer to increase the gift of God in us. God did not give us a spirit of fear, but instead it is our responsibility to receive from Him a spirit of power, love, and self-discipline.

Questions:

Who can I ask to pray for me to increase the gifts that God has given me... in my music and in my writing? If God did not give me a spirit of fear where is my fear coming from?

God answered: It is coming from the enemy.

Lord, how can I cultivate a spirit of power, love, and self-discipline?

Dr. Diana Wilcox

If I knew all of the wonderful things that God had waiting in store for me, would I be waiting and "camping out" like I am now?

Live in Response:

> Dear Lord,
>
> In the name of Jesus, I refuse to let any psychiatric label or other people's expectations or shame keep me from fulfilling your purpose for me. God bless the people in my family who have cast me aside, but I can't live my life to please them and to suit their expectations. I need to start living for you God. I claim God's promise for me now. Father, bring a right spirit to me, not one of timidity and fear, but a spirit of power, love, and self-discipline.
>
> Thank you God, I just want to serve you and to give glory and honor to you. It is my desire to bear fruit in your name. Forgive me for having been so timid, shy, and fearful. In the name of Jesus, I cast out that spirit of fear and negative thinking and I replace it with a spirit of love, power, and self-discipline. In the name of Jesus, I hereby stop camping out! I will

Thank God in Advance

call Bunny and ask him to pray for me. I commit to you Lord, that I will finish my book. Please, Lord, give me inspiration. Help me to write something truly useful and helpful and praising of God.

Thank you, Lord, for giving me more mental clarity and more courage in you. Lord, help me to make my testimony more moving, help me to describe all the wonderful benefits I have found in Jesus Christ now! Lord, thank you for showing me the vision you have for my life—the book, marketing both the book and the CD together by singing at public performances—not worrying about whether I have to look at the written words or not, and doing it all for the glory of God.

I am so grateful to Anne Graham Lotz for her encouragement and ability to give me a fresh glimpse of Jesus at the Just Give Me Jesus conference just last month! Her method of studying the Bible has proven invaluable to me! It has brought me closer to Jesus and has provided me with the courage to embrace God's vision for my life. Thank you God in advance for *all* the wonderful mercies that you will continue to show me day by day. Lord, you have answered my prayers: my prayers for the safety and happiness of my children, my prayers for a wonderful Christian husband, my prayers for dear friends, and my prayers to serve you through song and writing. You have taken away my fear of speaking and singing in public!

You have also answered my prayers to help me overcome my autism and the stigma of the label of Schizoaffective disorder. Of course I still take my medication religiously, because I have tried going off it before and it doesn't work! Thank you Lord for modern medicine and for my doctor and counselor! You are using my ability to overcome the autism and the psychiatric labels to encourage others and to glorify your name. You have also answered my prayer to increase my mental clarity and to start increasing my knowledge of your Word. You have answered my prayers to take care of my children.

You have answered my prayer to help me claim the Promised Land that you have mapped out for me with Jesus Christ! That you God! Thank God in advance!

Love, Diana

10-19-09

2 Corinthians 5:17

"Therefore, if anyone is in Christ, he is a new creation, the old as gone, the new has come!"

Lessons:

Anyone who is in Christ is a new creation. The old self has been cast off and the new has come.

Questions:

Do I accept myself as a new creation in Christ?
Have I fully said goodbye to my old self?
Have I been ready to say goodbye to my old self or has it been so comfortable that I have wanted to hang on?

Live in Response:

> Dear Lord,
> Help me to embrace the future you have planned for me by embracing myself as a new creation in Christ. Help me say goodbye to the old self.
>
> Love, Diana

10-20-09

Dear Lord,

I talked with my lawyer yesterday about radio promotion for the CD. It is extremely expensive, but I know that nothing is impossible for you.

Love, Diana

Matthew 6:12

I tell you the truth, if you have faith as small as a mustard seed, you can say to the mountain, move from here to there and it will move. Nothing will be impossible for you.

Lessons:

We need to believe Jesus that even with the smallest amount of faith, nothing will be impossible for us.

Questions:

Do I believe Jesus that even my small amount of faith will make everything possible for me?

Live in Response:

> Dear Lord,
> Let me completely trust in you and have faith in you so that with you nothing will be impossible for me.
>
> Love, Diana

Luke 1:34-38

34. "How will this be," Mary asked the angel, "since I am still a virgin?"

35. The angel answered, "The Holy Spirit will come upon you, and the power of the Most High will overshadow you. So the holy one to be born will be called the Son of God.

36. Even Elizabeth your relative is going to have a child in her old age, and she who is said to be barren is in her sixth month.

37. For nothing is impossible with God."

38. "I am the Lord's servant," Mary answered. "May it be to me as you have said." Then the angel left her.

Lessons:

34. Sometimes things seem impossible.
35. I was reading verse 35, and the Holy Spirit came over me, and I started speaking in tongues. An angel appeared to me as a soft voice. I kept my eyes closed. He said he was the angel Malachi and that I should read Malachi 8:2. He said, "You are the one who has been chosen to do this, to sing your songs." I said, "So be it." He told me to raise my hands high and to praise God. I raised my hands and praised God, Jesus, and the Holy Spirit, the three in one. I looked for Malachi 8:2, but there is no 8:2.

God said:

That just shows how much faith you have—that you looked it up! My word is important, but I am not the Bible and don't forget to spend time talking with me.

> Dear Lord,
> Thank you so much.
>
> Love, Diana

Thank God in Advance

God said to me:

> Diana,
>
> I would not have brought you this far just to abandon you without hope. I did not abandon the Israelites at the shore of the Red Sea when the Egyptian soldiers were chasing them and I won't abandon you. Go ahead and invest once the book is done. You will have a hit or two on your hands and will recoup your investment. You will get a double portion for your past shame. You have been faithful to me with what little you've had and I will be faithful to you.
>
> Plant your seed into your own ministry now! Halleluiah Diana! The time to harvest is now! Your harvest will be bountiful for you have passed the test and have much talent. Stay humble and always praise God.
>
> Love, God

Dear God,
I love you,

Diana

10-22-09

Genesis 22:11-15—Jehovah Jireh

11. But the angel of the Lord called out to him from heaven, "Abraham! Abraham!" "Here I am," he replied.
12. "Do not lay a hand on the boy," he said. "Do not do anything to him. Now I know that you fear God, because you have not withheld from me you son, your only son."
13. Abraham looked up and there in the thicket he saw a ram caught by its horns...
14. So Abraham called that place "The Lord Will Provide."

Lessons:

11. We need to listen for the angels of the Lord when we are tested.
12. God wants us to fully obey and revere Him and not to withhold anything that is precious to us from Him.
13. If we offer all that we have that is most precious to us to God, He will in turn give us what we need.

14. We need to remember that the Lord will provide for us.

Questions:

11. How often do I listen to hear an angel or God's voice when I am being tested?
12. Am I willing to devote all of my resources to God and to God's plan for my life?
13. Do I fully realize that if I devote all my resources to God's plan for my life, He will in turn provide for me?
14. Will I remember and express how the Lord has provided for me in my singing and my writing?

Live in Response:

> Dear Lord:
> Let me always listen for your voice, or an angel's voice during times when I am being tested.

Jesus said to me:

> I love you Diana with all my heart. I'm so glad you've come back to me fully. Take

care and love me with all your heart, mind, and strength. Fill your mind with love and you will be fine.

Love, Jesus

P.S. About your sins, my grace is enough for you!

Dear Lord,

Let me be willing to devote all of my resources wisely to God's plan for my life. Help me to be a good steward of my time, energy, and finances. Help me to realize that if I fully devote all my resources to your plan for my life, you will provide for me, for you are Jehovah Jireh! Praise God!

I proclaim abundance over my life! I proclaim the year of the Lord's favor. This time next year, people aren't going to recognize me. I proclaim it in Jesus's holy name! I love you Lord so much that I can hardly stand it! Forgive me, Father, for my past confusion and transgressions. I love you with my whole heart. I worship only you. You alone are worthy of my devotions and love. You alone hold the keys to my heart for eternity. God, Jesus, Holy Spirit, my friend, forgive me of my sins and welcome me as your friend for I love you with all that I am, can be and will ever be in your name!Halleluiah!

Tonight I am going to give a short testimony and sing three songs, Sweet Justice, Obstacles, and Cloak of Compassion at My Brother's Keeper, a homeless shelter here in Waco. Lord, let me do my best, and let me do it to glorify you.

Testimony for My Brother's Keeper:

Portions of this message were inspired by Pastor Paula White's CD, *Increase,* which I have listened to in the car over 300 times!

I was physically and sexually abused as a child. My father committed suicide when I was seventeen. I looked for love in all the wrong places. I lost custody of my first two children, because I had a nervous breakdown after being in an unhealthy relationship with my first husband. I've been diagnosed with autism and schizoaffective disorder. I've been homeless and in shelters before. Before I fully came to Christ at age forty-one, my life was an empty blur. I was lost, going from one bad relationship to another, looking for the love that only Jesus could give me.

I got saved watching the Trinity Broadcasting Network day in and day out on TV. God had arranged it so that it was the only station my little TV could get! If it weren't for Jesus coming into my life I would either be dead now or totally lost on the back wards of a psychiatric hospital somewhere.

Since I have given over every aspect of my life to God and am reading my Bible and spending time with Jesus every day, I am a new creation in Christ. I have joy and peace, and I love Jesus with all my heart, mind, and soul. I am reaping a harvest.

In John 4:35 Jesus says, "Do you not say 'four months more and then the harvest? I tell you, open your eyes and look at he fields! They are ripe for harvest!'" This means don't always say that your harvest is down the road. Look! Your harvest is ready now! Are you ready to reap the harvest that God has for you in your life?

I hereby come against the stigma of any diagnostic label or negative expectation that anybody has put on me or you in the past in the name of Jesus! I take captive of any negative thought in the name of Jesus! Your future will not be determined by your past!

Thank God in Advance

In Genesis 22:17, God was so pleased with Abraham that he said, "I will surely bless you and make your descendants as numerous as the stars in the sky and as the sand on the seashore. Your descendants will take possession of the cities of their enemies and through your offspring all nations of the earth will be blessed because you have obeyed me."

In other words, God said, you can thank me in advance for everything I am about to do for you, because you haven't seen anything yet. I'm going to open doors for you that no one can shut. It's your responsibility to walk through those doors and reap the harvest that God has waiting for you. I don't know who I came to prophesy to tonight, but you are going to have a harvest in your life that you won't be able to believe at first. You will be able to look back at this time and say that that was just a bump in the road. What the enemy meant to use as a stumbling block, God is going to use as a stepping-stone! Have courage! You can do all things through Christ!

To help me get through my suffering God dictated to me several songs that I either wrote down or sang into a hand-held tape recorder. These songs are now on a CD called *Thank God in Advance*. I am also writing a book called *Thank God in Advance* that complements the CD. Up until about a week ago, I was too shy and overburdened about the stigma of my diagnostic label to sing in public, but God had delivered me and given me a new voice. I'm now going to use that voice to sing some of God's songs of healing for you.

10-23-09

Revelation 15:1-5

1. I saw in heaven another great and marvelous sign: seven angels with the seven last plagues—last, because with them God's wrath is completed.

2. And I saw what looked like a sea of glass mixed with fire and standing beside the sea, those who had been victorious over the beast and his image and over the number of his name. They held harps given them by God

3. And sang the song of Moses the servant of God and the song of the Lamb:
"Great and marvelous are your deeds,
Lord God Almighty,

> Just and true are your ways,
> King of the ages.

4. Who will not fear you, O Lord,
   and bring glory to your name?
   For you alone are holy.
   All nations will come
   And worship before you,
   For your righteous acts have been revealed."

5. After this I looked and in heaven the temple, that is, the tabernacle of the Testimony was opened.

Lessons:

1. The wrath of God will be complete and final.

2. God's fury is like a sea of fire, and those who are victorious over evil will be given great rewards in heaven.

3. Those who have conquered evil will sing in heaven of the Lord's marvelous deeds.

4. We should fear the Lord and bring glory to His name for all nations will worship Him for His righteousness.

5. When we look to God He reveals His vision to us.

Questions:

1. Who can I warn others of the finality of God's wrath?

2. Am I sufficiently aware of God's fury? Am I ready to become even more victorious over evil so that I can reap a greater reward in heaven?

3. Am I willing to do battle with evil so that I can sing in heaven of the Lord's marvelous deeds?

4. Do I sufficiently fear and revere the Lord and bring glory to His name and help all nations worship Him for His righteousness?

5. Do I sufficiently look to God for my vision?

Live in Response:

> Dear Lord,
>
> Help me to be more aware of the finality and completeness of your fury. Help me to be more willing to battle evil more every day and to be victorious over evil so that I can lay my crown at your feet in heaven. Please increase my willingness to do battle with evil so that I can sing in heaven of your marvelous deeds. Help

Thank God in Advance

me to sufficiently fear and revere the Lord and to bring glory to your name and to help all nations to worship you for your righteousness! Lord, may this prayer be reflected in my songs and in my writing.

Love, Diana

10-24-09

Revelation 19:1-8

1. After this I heard what sounded like the roar of a great multitude in heaven shouting: "Hallelujah! Salvation and glory and power belong to our God,

2. For true and just are his judgments. He has condemned the great prostitute who corrupted the earth by her adulteries. He has avenged on her the blood of his servants."

3. Again they shouted, "Hallelujah! The smoke from her goes up for ever and ever."

4. The twenty-four elders and the four living creatures fell down and worshiped God, who

was seated on the throne. And they cried, "Amen, Hallelujah!"

5. Then a voice came from the throne, saying, "Praise our God, all you his servants, you who fear him, both small and great!"

6. Then I heard what sounded like a great multitude, like the roar of rushing waters and like loud peals of thunder, shouting, "Hallelujah! For our Lord God Almighty reigns.

7. Let us rejoice and be glad and give his glory! For the wedding of the Lamb has come, and his bride has made herself ready.

8. Fine linen, bright and clean, was given her to wear." (Fine linen stands for the righteous acts of the saints.)

Lessons:

1. The saints in heaven shout for joy in God's judgment for the salvation of the righteous and his punishment of evil.

2. Evil will be punished and those who fight evil will be rewarded.

3. The punishment of the wicked will be eternal.

Thank God in Advance

4. The Lord is worthy of worship and praise with all our hearts, minds, souls, and resources.
5. The Lord wants us to praise and fear Him no matter how small or great we may be.
6. When all the saints shout and praise God there is great power.
7. We should rejoice for it is time for Jesus to rejoin his church.
8. The saints will be given righteous acts to perform.

Questions:

1. How can I bring someone to salvation and cause heaven to rejoice through my singing and through my writing?
2. As I sing, am I willing to do battle with evil for the Lord?
3. Who can I warn of God's eternal punishment through my singing?
4. When I sing, am I truly worshiping and praising the Lord?
5. Do I listen to the Lord and praise and fear Him enough?

6. When I sing, do I allow myself to feel the great power of shouting for joy and praising God?

7. Have I made myself ready, like a bride, to rejoin Jesus? Why am I not always rejoicing then?

8. Will I be given righteous acts to perform by God? Can I look at my singing to those needing to hear the good news of God's Word as a righteous act?

Live in Response:

> Dear Lord,
> Thinking of how I can bring someone to salvation helps me feel less self-conscious about my singing. Help me to take the focus off myself and to put the focus solely on You and your glory. Help me bring others to salvation and cause heaven to rejoice through my singing. Allow me to be willing to do battle with evil for the Lord. Take me out of my comfort zone so that I may reap the harvest of souls you have waiting for me. Allow me to warn others, young and old,

rich and poor, male and female, of your eternal judgment through my singing.

Lord when I sing allow me to truly be in the moment and to truly worship and praise you. Allow me to feel and express your great power of shouting for joy and praising you.

Help me to make myself ready, Lord, in every way, in my singing, in my preparation, in my performing, in my testimony and in my writing. Help me to make myself ready to become your bride and to rejoin you in the second coming. Help me to rejoice in Jesus always.

Help me to see each opportunity to sing and each opportunity to give my testimony as an opportunity to perform a righteous act for you. Thank you God in advance for all the righteous acts you are going to allow me to perform in your name, bringing the good news of Jesus Christ to a lost world!

Love, Diana

PART FIVE
Pulling It All Together

You are a precious child of God. Whatever God has planned for you, you can attain. You just have to go out there and choose to walk through the door of opportunity that God will open for you. You can overcome emotional trauma, the stigma of diagnostic labels, a life of past sins, and other people's negative expectations of you. Your future is not determined by your past in God's eyes. It only matters where you're going!

It's okay to come broken to God; He uses the broken pieces of our lives to build a mosaic of future promises. Praise Him for being the God of all comfort and compassion. We can learn to have compassion for ourselves and for others. We need to fall in love with Jesus as the Lord of lords and the King of kings. We need to prepare ourselves as His bride in waiting for his second coming. We need to take care of ourselves physically, spiritually, mentally, and emotionally. This means fleeing from behavioral addictions and sexual immorality and devoting ourselves to God's service.

We need to practice self-discipline. This literally means making yourself into a disciple of Christ. Practice each of the fruits of the spirit: joy, peace, patience, faithfulness, love, self-control, kindness, and gentleness.

Pray with me: Lord, please help me to do my best to imitate Jesus Christ in all facets so that I may be like a jewel reflecting your perfect love. In Jesus's name, Amen.

Of all those who have ever walked the Earth, Jesus was the ultimate forgiver of sins. He said on the cross, "Father, forgive them for they do not know what they are doing" (Luke 23:34). In imitating Christ, we need to forgive others as He has so very generously forgiven us. You will come a long way in your healing once you have truly forgiven those who have hurt you. In fact the Bible says we need to bless those who have hurt us. Rejoice for them when something good happens for them and send them a card!

Once you are able to bless those who have hurt you, you will have more joy in your heart. God wants us to sing and praise Him in joy. When you realize that God has already won the victory in Jesus Christ's second coming, it is hard not to give praise to God Almighty for his glory!

On the road to your spiritual recovery, you need to stay humble in your service to others. This is the only way that God will be able to advance you. Also as you know that trouble will come, you need to learn to put on the full armor of God (Ephesians 6:10-17). This will protect you from the snares of the enemy. Additionally, you need to overcome your fears as God promises to always be with you. Once you have taken these steps you will begin to be able to develop your own spiritual gifts.

Most importantly, spend time with God and Jesus. Read your Bible daily. Pray as much as possible and keep a daily prayer journal. A journal can be an invaluable record to you of God's answers to your prayers. It will bolster your faith enormously! You will see yourself progress from one view of your life to a totally new vision for your life in Jesus Christ!

PART SIX
Receive God's Vision For Your Life

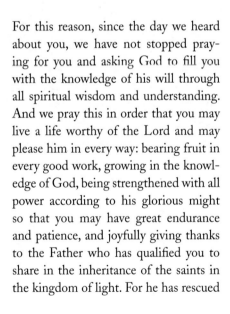

For this reason, since the day we heard about you, we have not stopped praying for you and asking God to fill you with the knowledge of his will through all spiritual wisdom and understanding. And we pray this in order that you may live a life worthy of the Lord and may please him in every way: bearing fruit in every good work, growing in the knowledge of God, being strengthened with all power according to his glorious might so that you may have great endurance and patience, and joyfully giving thanks to the Father who has qualified you to share in the inheritance of the saints in the kingdom of light. For he has rescued

> us from the dominion of darkness and
> brought us into the kingdom of the Son
> he loves, in whom we have redemption,
> the forgiveness of sins.
>
> Colossians 1:9-13

In this verse Paul prays for us that God will fill us with the knowledge of His will through all spiritual wisdom and understanding. He prays that we will live a life worthy of the Lord and please Him in every way.

Pray with me: Lord, let me receive knowledge of your will through your spiritual wisdom so that I may live a life worthy of you. Help me to receive your vision for my life. Help me to bear fruit in every good work and to grow in the knowledge of you. Let me be strengthened with all power so that I may have endurance and patience and joyfully give thanks to you God. Allow me to live a life worthy of the price that you paid in sending your Son to redeem our sins and to bring us into the kingdom of light. I pray for new vision for my life Lord as I draw closer to you. Let whatever you would have me do be to the glory of you and you alone. In Jesus's name, Amen.

Thank God in Advance

Once you have a clear vision for your life from Jesus, it is much easier to live your life because you have a map to follow! "Without a vision, the people perish (Proverbs 29:18)." This means that a vision is so vital that you can lose your faith and your very life with out it. Pray every day that God will give you a clear vision for your life, and guide you accordingly.

I would either be dead or in the back ward of a psychiatric hospital somewhere if it weren't for Jesus in my life. He has given me a vision and a hope. He has rescued me from danger and set me on solid ground. I cannot thank Him enough for His mercies. Every day as I draw closer to Jesus, His vision for my life becomes clearer and I know that I need to serve only Him. I pray the same for you dear reader.

PART SEVEN
Sing a New Song to The Lord

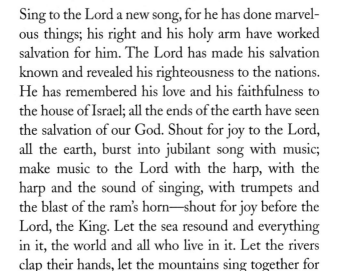

Sing to the Lord a new song, for he has done marvelous things; his right and his holy arm have worked salvation for him. The Lord has made his salvation known and revealed his righteousness to the nations. He has remembered his love and his faithfulness to the house of Israel; all the ends of the earth have seen the salvation of our God. Shout for joy to the Lord, all the earth, burst into jubilant song with music; make music to the Lord with the harp, with the harp and the sound of singing, with trumpets and the blast of the ram's horn—shout for joy before the Lord, the King. Let the sea resound and everything in it, the world and all who live in it. Let the rivers clap their hands, let the mountains sing together for joy; let them sing before the Lord, for he comes to judge he earth. He will judge the righteousness and the peoples with equity (Psalm 98).

We can sing and be happy for in the end Jesus will come and rule over the world. God will finally be with all of us. He will wipe every tear from our eyes. Suffering and death will be gone and the old order of things will pass away (See Revelation 21:4). He will make everything new! God will allow everyone who is thirsty to drink from the spring of the water of life. Whoever overcomes will be considered his son or daughter. God's justice will be done. What a wonderful time it will be! How can we be sad or worried knowing that the world is in God's mighty hands? He has already won the victory!

If God can win the battle over the entire universe, surely he can take care of you. Have faith in Him and put your trust in the Lord, rather than in your own strength and understanding. "Trust in the Lord with all your heart and lean not on your own understanding; in all your ways acknowledge him, and he will make your paths straight" (Proverbs 3:5-6).

Sing a new song of praise to the Lord thanking him in advance for all the marvelous works that he is about to do in your life. By this time next year, people aren't going to recognize you! God will have performed a miracle in your life! If he can do it for me, he can do it for you! Shout for joy to the Lord!

Thank God in Advance

For you will have abundance! I prophesy an abundant harvest of souls for you for the Lord's glory in Jesus Christ! You will wear a crown in heaven, and you will be able to lay that beautiful crown at the feet of Jesus!